Grammar Survival for Primary Teachers

Are you grappling with grammar? Are you perplexed by punctuation? Do you find it a constant challenge to keep your pupils engaged while teaching grammar effectively?

Focusing on what you need to know in the classroom, *Grammar Survival for Primary Teachers* provides you with all of the knowledge and practical advice you'll need to teach grammar and punctuation effectively. Based on a successful, tried-and-tested format, this new book is designed especially for primary teachers and focuses on the requirements of the English National Curriculum for Key Stages 1 and 2.

This book includes:

- clear explanations and examples of a range of different aspects of grammar and punctuation
- practical advice and teaching ideas for use in the classroom
- a strong focus on building knowledge and applying it to writing.

Accessible and engaging, this new book will be essential reading for busy trainee, newly qualified and practising teachers alike. It is the perfect guide for those looking to improve both their pupils' and their own understanding of grammar.

Jo Shackleton has been a teacher, consultant and inspector. She has been a curriculum adviser on the grammar, punctuation and spelling (GPS) tests and has worked at a national level on the teacher assessment and moderation of writing at Key Stage 2. She has also provided training to primary teachers throughout the country on grammar and punctuation.

Grammar Survival for Primary Teachers

A Practical Toolkit

Jo Shackleton

Routledge
Taylor & Francis Group

LONDON AND NEW YORK

First published 2017
by Routledge
2 Park Square, Milton Park, Abingdon, Oxon OX14 4RN

and by Routledge
711 Third Avenue, New York, NY 10017

Routledge is an imprint of the Taylor & Francis Group, an informa business

British Library Cataloguing in Publication Data
A catalogue record for this book is available from the British Library

Library of Congress Cataloging in Publication Data
A catalog record for this book has been requested

ISBN: 978-1-138-28461-6 (hbk)
ISBN: 978-1-138-28462-3 (pbk)
ISBN: 978-1-315-26937-5 (ebk)

Typeset in Minion Pro
by Swales & Willis Ltd, Exeter, Devon, UK

Printed and bound in Great Britain by
TJ International Ltd, Padstow, Cornwall

Contents

Acknowledgements

I'm indebted to two valued colleagues: Margaret Fennell has acted as a critical friend throughout the drafting of this book, and her forensic approach to detail has been invaluable; Geoff Barton, who approached me with the idea for this book, has provided overwhelming support and positive feedback throughout. I'm very grateful to them both.

Foreword

Grammar is one of those topics that – like spiders, snakes, enclosed spaces, clowns and rats – can terrify many of us. Even those of us who reckon we are pretty assured in our knowledge of how language works can suddenly become spooked by another person's comment, criticism or act of linguistic one-upmanship.

That's made harder when there's a national agenda to teach grammar, spelling and punctuation much more explicitly to children of a much younger age. It makes the teaching of grammar seem much higher-stakes – whether we believe the prescribed approach is right or misguided.

That's why I love Jo Shackleton's *Grammar Survival for Primary Teachers* so much.

First, it goes straight to the heart of what language knowledge will help young children to read and, in particular, write more effectively. Based on her huge experience, Jo knows this stuff, and she is passionate in her belief that certain concepts, terminology and approaches will liberate our pupils to communicate with greater clarity and precision.

She gives us, in other words, a crystal clear rationale for making grammatical knowledge more explicit.

Then she writes in a tone which is never patronizing, always accessible and which leaves even the most insecure of us feeling that there are ideas here that are unignorable, inclusive and manageable by each of us in every classroom.

The format of the book reinforces this clarity. What you need to know is on the left-hand page; how you might use that knowledge in your teaching is on the right. It's the perfect example of moving from relevant knowledge to practical application.

I couldn't be more proud to be associated with this book. I think it's an important, must-have text for every teacher – for those working in primary schools and for those who then welcome these same children into our lower secondary classrooms, determined to maintain the momentum of learning.

Thanks to Jo for this essential guide to making grammar powerfully effective in our primary schools. I hope you find it as helpful, reassuring and ultimately inspiring as I have.

Geoff Barton
Suffolk
November 2016

Introduction

In 2014, we saw the introduction of the new primary national curriculum. Its statutory assessment and its more challenging grammar, punctuation and spelling content have raised the stakes in terms of what teachers need to know about grammar and punctuation.

As primary teachers, you have to know a lot of things about a lot of subjects – not just grammar – so it's not surprising if you feel there may be gaps in your own subject knowledge. After all, many of us weren't taught grammar at school, and the National Literacy Strategy's 'Grammar for Writing' materials are a distant memory for many.

What's more, some of the familiar terminology has shifted: connectives (that useful 'catch-all' term) have vanished without trace; articles have been incorporated into determiners; and simple and complex sentences are described in terms of single-clause and multi-clause sentences.

There's a clear grammatical rationale for all of this – but we could be forgiven for feeling just a little bit insecure.

The grammatical content that must be taught is set out in the national curriculum programmes of study and its statutory appendices. This book deals with that content, as well as one or two other aspects that aren't statutory (such as non-finite clauses) because they are interesting in their own right and may well help your pupils to become better writers if they know how to deploy them effectively.

Grammar Survival for Primary Teachers aims to support your subject knowledge in an easy-to-use way. Each left-hand page sets out the knowledge you need about different aspects of grammar and punctuation. But it goes further in that it aims to support your pedagogical knowledge too. I've met many very good teachers who've told me that grammar is boring and hard. They're unsure how to teach it in engaging and creative ways. Many are teaching it discretely, devoid of any meaningful application in writing, simply to make sure that it gets covered. That's understandable, but we know that independent application in writing is the real test of embedded learning. So each right-hand page deals with application, offering practical ideas and approaches for teaching grammar and punctuation in the classroom.

Personally, I believe the increased emphasis on grammar and punctuation is no bad thing. I don't believe it's boring, or that it stifles creativity. I don't believe that we have to choose between knowledge about grammar and punctuation on the one side, or creativity on the other. I do believe that children can – and should – have both. To have both is better – knowledge *and* application – not one or the other. Knowledge about grammar and punctuation, engagingly and effectively taught, can give young writers the tools they need to make conscious choices about their writing, so that they can be both creative *and* in control.

The teaching ideas in this book are approaches rather than activities, so you can adapt them to suit your class and the children in it. Some of the grammar introduced in Key Stage 1 needs to be developed and consolidated in Key Stage 2 so you can take the approaches and think about how they might work with younger or older pupils in your school.

There are five important points to make about the teaching approaches in this book:

1. They're informed and underpinned by research, so we know they work. You may well have encountered them before:

   - 'hands-on' inductive approaches that draw out the implicit knowledge about language that children have in abundance
   - investigative approaches that enable children to work out rules and conventions for themselves, giving them ownership of their learning
   - 'sentence-combining' approaches that enable children to experiment with and manipulate clauses to explore syntactic choices
   - 'creative imitation' approaches that enable children to borrow from reading and to learn from experienced writers.

   This final approach ('creative imitation') is, I believe, a really powerful one: it's an apprentice model, whereby young writers internalise the patterns of language, trying them on for size, before adapting and importing them into their own writing.

2. They recognise the importance of talk – and talk about language – including grammar. Very young pupils talk happily about phonemes and graphemes, and there's no reason why children in Key Stages 1 and 2 shouldn't use other grammatical language to talk about their own reading and writing.

3. They are based on the premise that reading informs writing. However, we know that children don't always make this connection naturally, and that's why explicit (rather than discrete) teaching is key. Drawing on the rich reading experiences in your classroom; exploring texts through shared reading; sharing a model and teasing out the writer's technique and choices and the way they impact on the reader – these are all key to the effective teaching of grammar.

4. They endorse the importance of modelled, shared and guided writing. Modelling short pieces of writing and thinking aloud as you write; deliberating on and orally rehearsing your choices; inviting pupils to share the composition with you, sifting and challenging their contributions – these fundamental approaches continue to underpin the teaching of writing because they make the writing process visible. Guided writing – working with small groups of pupils to move them, through supported application, to independence – is a key element of this pedagogy.

5. They maintain a focus on teaching grammar and punctuation in the context of reading and writing across the curriculum, supporting the view that knowledge about grammar can help children to become better and more confident readers and writers, whatever the subject or topic.

Of course, once you've taught about grammar and punctuation, you'll want to make sure that your pupils have opportunities to apply their knowledge in meaningful contexts. Some teachers call this 'smart planning'. For example, if you've taught about the passive voice, you'll want to make sure that you develop writing opportunities whereby pupils need to use it. That's why there's a short paragraph in each section that explains when we might need to use particular aspects of grammar and punctuation in our writing.

There's also a glossary and further recommended reading at the end.

I hope you find it helpful.

Jo Shackleton
October 2016

What you need to know about word classes

This chapter deals with the eight main word classes: nouns, verbs (including verb forms and modal verbs), adjectives, adverbs, prepositions, determiners, conjunctions and pronouns. Some people refer to word classes as 'parts of speech', although word class is generally considered to be a more helpful term.

The really important thing to be aware of is that many words can function as more than one word class, so it is often simply not possible to say that X is a noun or Y is an adverb. It all depends on how the word is used in a sentence. This is why we tend to talk about a word's <u>function</u>.

To see what this looks like in practice, consider the following:

1. I struck a <u>match</u> to light the fire. 2. My dad took me to my first football <u>match</u>. 3. Her jacket didn't really <u>match</u> her trousers. 'Match' functions as a noun in the first two sentences, although it has a different meaning in each. However, in the third sentence it functions as a verb.	1. As I looked into the sky, I heard the long, low <u>cry</u> of a seagull. 2. 'Please don't <u>cry</u>. It's only a scratch.' In the first sentence, 'cry' functions as a noun; in the second, it functions as a verb.
1. Our house has a <u>downstairs</u> cloakroom, which is really handy whenever we have visitors. 2. She ran <u>downstairs</u> when she heard the knock at the door. 'Downstairs' functions as an adjective in the first sentence, modifying the noun 'cloakroom'. In the second sentence, it functions as an adverb, modifying the verb 'ran'.	1. <u>Before </u>I learnt to play the trumpet, I could only play a few notes on the recorder. 2. We always finish choir practice <u>before</u> 7 o'clock so that we can get home in time for supper. In the first sentence, 'before' functions as a subordinating conjunction to introduce a subordinate clause. In the second sentence, it functions as a preposition to introduce the preposition phrase 'before 7 o'clock'.
1. <u>This</u> story is definitely one of your best! 2. <u>This</u> is simply not good enough! 3. 'Yuk! What's <u>this</u>?' Billy asked rudely. In the first sentence, 'this' functions as a determiner to specify the noun 'story'. However, in the second and third sentences, it functions as a demonstrative pronoun to 'point to' something outside of the sentence.	1. The sound of the <u>dripping</u> tap kept me awake all night. 2. The tap was <u>dripping</u> and the door was hanging off its hinges. In the first sentence, 'dripping' functions as an adjective to modify the noun 'tap'. In the second sentence, it functions as the –ing form of the verb 'drip' to form the past progressive ('was dripping').

Teaching about word classes

Because many words don't sit neatly in one single word class, it's important to teach words in context rather than through decontextualised exercises. Wherever possible, it's best to make use of opportunities to explore the way words are used in high-quality texts as part of the reading curriculum, and in children's own writing.

Although you won't necessarily want to interrupt the enjoyment of a good story to explore the use of – say – nouns or adjectives, there's no problem with pausing every now and then to savour a really good sentence or apt choice of word. Good readers do this intuitively, having internalised the process over time. It's important that you model this 'readerly' behaviour for your pupils, perhaps through shared or guided reading as you explore a text with your class.

Other ways of encouraging pupils to notice the way writers create striking images or telling description through their choice of words include annotating a text with two or three sticky notes, using symbols such as exclamation marks or smiley faces. This has the benefit of not interrupting the flow of the reading, and pupils can return to them later in discussion. Alternatively, you could use a cloze exercise in reverse by giving them a handful of nouns, verbs, adjectives or adverbs from a text and asking them to predict the theme or storyline before reading it.

When introducing word classes to younger children, you might give them a handful of words, colour-coded according to word class, and ask them to use them to make as many phrases or sentences as they can. Once they've done this, ask them what they notice about the words on different coloured card. *What do all the words on the green cards do? And what do all the words on the blue cards do?* Then you can introduce the terminology, once pupils have an understanding of how the words work in practice. (You can limit or increase the number of words you provide, and give fewer word classes at a time if you wish.)

This type of inductive approach has the benefit of drawing on pupils' existing (but implicit) knowledge, as well as being very 'hands-on' and potentially collaborative. There's an example in the grid below to give you an idea, but you can make your own. You might want to link it thematically to a topic you've been studying or a subject of particular interest to your class.

he	we	they	she	you	I
a	an	the	some	each	every
sand	children	sky	seagull	beach	water
played	screamed	danced	splashed	flew	laughed
blue	warm	noisy	playful	happy	hopeful
lazily	carelessly	slowly	hungrily	wildly	playfully
in	on	under	beneath	over	behind
if	so	because	as	and	but

Some word classes are introduced in Key Stage 1, with others following in lower Key Stage 2. However, there are opportunities to teach older pupils how to build on this knowledge by using nouns for greater precision when writing in a more formal style, or by using adverbs to indicate a writer's stance.

What you need to know about nouns

It's difficult to give a simple and satisfactory definition of a noun. The idea of a 'naming' word is not completely helpful, although it's true that nouns do help us to name and reference the world around us. Nouns are words that indicate things, including people, places, events, qualities and ideas. They typically have a singular and a plural form.

These are all nouns:

library	patience	Edinburgh	fox cub
football	Brighton	satisfaction	moment
Manchester United	teacher	staircase	history

Nouns can be modified by determiners, adjectives, phrases and clauses. They can function as the 'head' of a noun phrase (we'll look at this later in the chapter on phrases).

There are different classes of noun, including the following:

- Proper nouns name specific people, places, events or things, such as Elm Road, Sally Smith or the Atlantic Ocean. The days of the week and months of the year fall into this category, as do brand names. Proper nouns begin with a capital letter and don't normally take a plural form.

- Concrete nouns are a type of common noun. These name things that can be observed or quantified, such as computers, books, cattle or pictures.

- Abstract nouns are another type of common noun. These denote abstract qualities, ideas or concepts – things that cannot be seen or touched, such as fear, kindness, horror or importance.

There is another type of noun worth mentioning here because of the way it can take a singular or plural verb: 'human' collective nouns, such as staff, committee, team and family can take either a plural or a singular verb, depending on whether you want to emphasise the collective group or the individuals within it. The following would all be correct, depending on the writer's intention:

- The school staff are choosing the furniture for the new staffroom.
- The school staff is choosing the furniture for the new staffroom.
- The class are holding a party.
- The class is holding a party.

There are various suffixes that can be used to form nouns. The national curriculum specifies –er (teacher), –ness (kindness), –ment (enjoyment) and –ation (information), but there are many more, such as –ship (friendship), –hood (motherhood) and –ity (enmity). There are also suffixes that can be added to concrete nouns to signify gender (waiter/waitress, actor/actress) and size (duck/duckling, book/booklet).

Teaching about nouns

Help pupils to think about the way nouns function in a text by giving them a piece of 'nonsense' text to read. You could use 'Jabberwocky' from *Through the Looking-Glass and What Alice Found There* by Lewis Carroll, or you could make up your own. (When introducing nouns to younger children, you could create a passage based on a traditional tale.) Ask pupils to decide which 'nonsense' words are functioning as nouns, and ask them to explain how they know. Discussion might focus on the determiners and adjectives that precede the nouns, and the use of capital letters to denote proper nouns.

> The little **brog** breeped grappily at the **Drablad**. It sliggled past the ribbly **pladgers** and sklattered down the brumbly **bopes**. It came to a diggly **dop** when it saw the huge **Wiggersnap**.

Share sentence cards where the same word functions as a noun and another word class. Give pupils 'show me' cards to indicate when the word is used as a noun. Ask them to explain how they know.

The players ran onto the football <u>pitch</u>.	It was <u>pitch</u> dark outside, and it had been raining.	She decided to <u>pitch</u> her tent in the field.

Alternatively, you could explore homonyms (words that have the same spelling but different meanings). Homonyms tend to function as different word classes, but you could challenge pupils to think of homonyms that function as nouns with different meanings.

Show pupils how nouns – especially proper nouns – can create precision in writing. It can be very effective to name a thing specifically instead of relying on adjectives, phrases and clauses to modify it. Compare the following:

- The man drove down the lane in his little red open-top sports car.
- The man drove down the lane in his red Mercedes.

Pie Corbett refers to this as 'naming it', a key concept using precise nouns to create a powerful picture for the reader. It's the difference between 'dog' and 'mastiff', or 'dog' and 'Chihuahua'. You'll think of other examples. This is best done through modelled writing and shared composition, so that you can articulate the choices you are making as a writer, and support pupils as they do the same.

When teaching pupils to write in a more formal style, it's worth teaching them about nominalisation (or 'nouniness' as it's occasionally described). Nominalisation means forming a noun from another word class – usually a verb or an adjective. This is a particularly good way of helping pupils to write in a crisper, more succinct and formal style. Compare the following:

- Parents **were concerned** when the headteacher <u>resigned</u>.
- The <u>resignation</u> of the headteacher caused much **concern**.

WHEN MIGHT WE NEED TO USE NOUNS IN WRITING?

Nouns help us to name and reference the world around us so we can't really manage without them. It's possible, though, to help your pupils use them in more precise, varied and interesting ways in their writing. In non-fiction writing, particularly in subjects like science that have their own technical vocabulary, the precise and accurate choice of nouns is essential.

What you need to know about verbs and verb forms

Just as it's not particularly helpful to call a noun a 'naming' word, neither is it particularly helpful to refer to verbs as 'doing' words. Verbs don't only indicate action: they denote states of being as well, and this is particularly true of the verbs *be*, *do* and *have*. Think about the following, where there is no apparent action or 'doing' at all:

> I <u>am</u> hungry.
> The restaurant <u>is</u> on the beach.
> I <u>have</u> a bad cold.

There are three types of verb:

1. Lexical verbs are sometimes referred to as 'content' verbs, as they typically depict actions, events and states:
   - Harry <u>rode</u> his bike to football practice.
   - We <u>trudged</u> along the footpath until we <u>arrived</u>, exhausted, at the hostel.
   - We <u>remained</u> good friends.

2. Auxiliary verbs (be, do, have) are sometimes referred to as 'helper' or 'helping' verbs. Like lexical verbs, they can stand on their own as a main verb (I <u>have</u> a headache), but they more usually appear in a supportive (auxiliary) role in front of a lexical verb:
   - I <u>have</u> just thought of a great idea.
   - We <u>do</u> enjoy the summer holidays.
   - Zara <u>was</u> training for a half marathon.

   Auxiliary verbs are used to make other verb forms, such as the progressive and the perfect forms, as well as the passive.

3. Modal verbs are a type of auxiliary verb. We'll look at these more closely in the next section.

With the exception of modal verbs, verbs can take different forms.

- The base form is also referred to as the infinitive form (watch/to watch, sleep/to sleep, be/to be).
- The –s form is used to form the simple present in the third-person singular (she laughs, it rains, Jack sighs).
- The –ed form is used to form the simple past (they laughed, it rained, we sighed) as well as the –ed participle (sometimes referred to as the past participle), which is used to form the present and past perfect (they have laughed, it has rained, Jack had sighed) as well as the passive voice (the window was smashed). The –ed form can also form adjectives (the darkened room, a smashed window) and non-finite verbs (we'll explore these later in the chapter on clauses). Remember that the –ed form of irregular verbs may vary (swim, swam, swum/sing, sang, sung).
- The –ing form (sometimes referred to as the present participle) is used to form the present and past progressive (Jack is sighing; it was raining). Like the –ed form, it can also form adjectives (the boiling water, a promising start) and non-finite verbs. It can also form the gerund, a verb that functions as a noun (eating is not allowed in the library; swimming is good exercise).

Multi-word verbs (including phrasal and prepositional verbs) such as *pick up, find out, get away with* tend to be used in more informal writing and speech.

Apart from the –ed and –ing suffixes, which make grammatical changes to the verb, there are other suffixes that can be used to form verbs from other word classes. These include –ate (generate), –ise (liquidise), –ify (verify) and –en (lengthen).

Teaching about verbs and verb forms

When writing for different purposes and audiences across a range of forms, it's important to show pupils which tense and verb forms are likely to be most appropriate. At Key Stage 1, you'll be concerned primarily with the simple past and present and the progressive form; at Key Stage 2, you'll also be looking at the perfect form (past and present) as well as combined forms such as the past perfect progressive (we *had been hoping* to raise enough to. . .). Here are some examples:

A book review	Simple present to give opinion: . . .the story **is** really funny and the little fox **is** so cute. . . Simple past to describe events in the book: . . .the best bit **was** when the fox first **saw** the snow. . .
A write-up of a science experiment	Range of past tense forms: . . .first we **connected** the copper wire to the. . . . . .we **had** already **tested** the connection between. . .
A story	Range of past tense forms for narration: . . .the climber **heard** the rumble of thunder, but since he **had** already **checked** the weather forecast. . . Present tense for any dialogue: . . .'Watch out! **It's starting** to fall!'. . .
An autobiography	Range of past tense forms for memories: . . .I **had** always **been** an adventurous child. . . . . .we **grew up** on a farm. . . Present perfect for current reflection: . . .I **have** always **thought** of myself as a survivor. . .
A newspaper report	Range of forms, including past perfect, infinitive form, past perfect progressive and modals, to indicate the time frame of events: . . .the robbers **had waited** for the bank **to close**. . . . . .the manager **had been locking** the safe when. . . . . .the police **would like to hear** from anybody who. . . Present tense for journalistic comment: . . .this **is** the fifth burglary this month. . . . . .the recent crime wave **is** a cause for concern. . .
An information text	Simple present to give information: . . .whales **are** mammals that **live** in the sea. . .
A persuasive letter	Simple present and present progressive to state the current situation: . . .so we really **need** some new playground equipment. . . . . .we **are using** the old equipment which **is**n't very good. . . Past progressive and perfect forms: . . .as we **were hoping** to raise enough to. . . . . .we **have raised** enough to buy. . .

Sometimes, pupils tend to switch inappropriately from past to present (or vice versa) in their writing, especially if they get carried away with a strong narrative thread in a story, or don't have a firm grasp of a particular text type. If this is the case with your pupils, it's worth exploring it explicitly as a class activity. You might display a piece of writing on a visualiser and model how to edit for tense consistency. We'll revisit this in the chapter on cohesion.

WHEN MIGHT WE NEED TO USE VERBS AND VERB FORMS IN WRITING?

Writers need to use a range of verb forms most of the time, and increasingly so in writing across the curriculum, deploying different text types for different purposes and audiences.

What you need to know about modal verbs

Modality relates to the way a speaker or writer expresses attitudes such as possibility, certainty, necessity and ability. This is largely achieved through modal verbs, but some adverbs and their related nouns and adjectives can do this too (probably, in all probability, it is probable that. . .).

There are nine core modal verbs:

- can
- could
- may
- might
- must
- shall
- should
- will
- would

Some grammarians also recognise *dare*, *ought to*, *need* and *used to* as semi (or marginal) modals.

Unlike lexical verbs, and the three auxiliary verbs (be, do, have), modal verbs cannot take any other form: they cannot take an –s form, an –ed form or an –ing form. They exist in one form only.

Like the auxiliary verbs, their negative is formed by using *not* – or a contracted *n't* – (would not/ wouldn't). There are three irregular negative forms: cannot, shan't and won't.

Modals express shades of meaning related to possibility, probability and certainty. Consider the difference in meaning created by the modals in the following two sentences:

- I will tidy my room in a moment.
- I might tidy my room in a moment.

Modals also carry meaning related to permission, obligation and compulsion:

- May I tidy my room now?
- I should really tidy my room now.
- You really must tidy your room now.

The meanings carried by modal verbs can be quite subtle – and open to interpretation, dependent on context. Does the following sentence mean that Fred is able to read his story (he has the skill and the ability to do so) or that he is being given permission to read his story?

- Fred can read his story now.

Modals can be associated with politeness, adding an element of tentativeness to soften a directive:

- Would you pass the sauce?
- Might I have a word?
- We ought to be thinking about getting ready soon.

And – in the absence of a specific future tense – they allow us to refer to future time:

- I shall never forget what you have done for us.
- One day, we will look back on all of this and laugh about it.
- They'll be arriving in about half an hour.

Teaching about modal verbs

Modal verbs don't appear in the national curriculum until year 5. Although pupils are almost certain to have used them from a much younger age, they are less likely to understand the range and subtlety of meaning they express. This is, perhaps, the richest area to be explored at Key Stage 2. It can be teased out and taught at sentence level, but should then be contextualised and embedded in meaningful language study and use – through talking, reading and writing.

Give pupils a sentence and ask them to try out different modal verbs to see what difference they make to the meaning:

- Petra should/may/will/can/must go home tomorrow.
- Will/would/could you open the window?

Give pupils a short text, such as an invitation, and ask them to use modals to make it sound more polite (and formal):

Please come to my party on Thursday at 4 o'clock. Food is provided, and games are planned outside, weather permitting. Please reply by the end of the week.

I would be pleased if you could come to my party on Thursday. It will start at 4 o'clock. Food will be provided, and there may be games in the garden, weather permitting. Please would you reply by the end of the week? I do hope you can come!

Alternatively, give pupils a text and ask them to fill in the gaps with the most appropriate modal verbs. You might also introduce some adverbs that express modality. Pupils could work in groups to convey different attitudes, e.g. remorseful, resentful, mischievous, etc.

Dear Mrs Brown

I am writing to apologise for breaking your greenhouse window yesterday.

I _____ _____ pay for the damage and _____ _____ be more careful when I play football in our garden.

can	could	may	certainly	possibly	definitely
might	must	shall	obviously	surely	clearly
should	will	would	probably	perhaps	apparently

WHEN MIGHT WE NEED TO USE MODAL VERBS IN WRITING?

It's actually quite difficult to avoid using modals in writing as they enable writers to express their attitude (or stance), particularly relating to intentions or 'truths' about events that haven't yet happened.

What you need to know about adjectives

Adjectives are sometimes referred to as 'describing' words, but this is no more helpful than refer-ring to a verb as a 'doing' word, or a noun as a 'naming' word. It's more helpful to think about the way an adjective functions in a sentence.

Adjectives give more information about nouns and pronouns. We often talk about adjectives 'modifying' a noun.

- The <u>little</u> cottage sat in the middle of the <u>magical</u> forest.
- She was <u>lonely</u> without her friends.
- The teacher rode his <u>rusty</u>, <u>old</u> bike to school.

They typically come immediately before a noun, where they are called attributive adjectives:

- It was a <u>sunny</u> day.
- The <u>bright</u>, <u>colourful</u> flowers swayed in the <u>gentle</u> breeze.
- The <u>old</u> fisherman looked out at the <u>rough</u> sea.

However, adjectives can appear in other positions too:

- The day, <u>sunny</u> and <u>warm</u>, started well.
- The flowers swaying in the breeze were <u>bright</u> and <u>colourful</u>.
- The sea was <u>rough</u>.

Some adjectives are gradable, which means they express qualities that are variable. (Just how hot is that hot water?) These adjectives have comparative and superlative forms. In many cases, these are formed by adding –er and –est (large/larger/largest), but some have completely different forms (good/better/best). Some take more/most (beautiful/more beautiful/most beautiful).

A note of warning: some comparative and superlative adjectives can also function as comparative and superlative adverbs.

Sometimes a noun is modified by another noun (a <u>cheese</u> sandwich/the <u>school</u> <u>sports</u> day). Although these seem to function as adjectives, they are still nouns and are referred to as attributive nouns.

Adjectives have a key role to play in expanding noun phrases, and we'll look at this in the chapter on phrases.

There are various suffixes that can be used to form adjectives. The national curriculum references –ful (hopeful), –less (careless) and –ous (generous), but there are many others, such as –ive (expensive), –ish (childish), –al (accidental) and –y (sunny).

Teaching about adjectives

Once younger pupils have been taught about adjectives, they sometimes have a tendency to overuse them. This might look familiar: the <u>ugly, old, nasty</u> witch cackled as she cast her spell. . . The most descriptive word here is arguably *cackled*! When this happens, it's important to focus on the strengths of the writing: the issue will resolve itself as young writers become more assured and have more 'writerly' tools at their disposal.

The best way to explore the use of adjectives is to discuss them as part of the reading curriculum. Any high-quality text by an established children's writer will provide rich opportunities for exploration and discussion, and you will find plenty of whole-class and small-group opportunities through shared and guided reading as part of your day-to-day teaching.

Even though adjectives feature in year 2 of the national curriculum, there are plenty of opportunities to explore their use with older pupils too. As part of your study of fiction from our literary heritage in years 5/6, you may well be reading a novel like 'Treasure Island'. If so, you might ask the class to consider the way Stevenson uses adjectives to present the island through the eyes of the young Jim Hawkins in this passage:

> Grey-coloured woods covered a large part of the surface. This even tint was indeed broken up by streaks of yellow sandbreak in the lower lands, and by many tall trees of the pine family, out-topping the others – some singly, some in clumps; but the general colouring was uniform and sad.

Alternatively, you could give pupils a cloze passage and ask them to think of suitable adjectives to complete the gaps. The most obvious way is to take an extract from a book you are reading with the class. This type of activity is best done in pairs or small groups, so that pupils can share their ideas with each other. It's important not to present the original version as the 'right' answer: use it to explore the different choices that writers make and the effect of those language choices on the reader. If pupils need more support with this type of activity, you can always give them a bank of words to choose from.

> . . .the _____ river flowed easily through the _____ valley, winding its way to the sea. It looked _____ and _____.

If you're working on synonyms, you could give pupils a collection of related adjectives (use a good thesaurus to find them) and ask them to arrange them on a continuum. This is a great approach for discussing the way words carry shades of meaning – since there is no clear answer, it's likely to promote rich discussion.

cold	icy	glacial	chilly	cool	arctic	freezing

WHEN MIGHT WE NEED TO USE ADJECTIVES IN WRITING?

Adjectives are essential whenever we want to add descriptive detail to writing. They are of particular use in narrative, when establishing setting and characterisation. They're important in factual writing too, if we need to classify a noun to be more precise and specific.

What you need to know about adverbs

Adverbs can be tricky, because they can be used in such a wide range of ways. Their main function is to modify verbs, but they can also modify adjectives, or other adverbs. They also function adverbially when they form part of a phrase or clause, but we'll look at this in the chapter on phrases and clauses.

You may see adverbs grouped in different ways according to their meaning, but the following groups are widely agreed:

Adverbs of time (including frequency and duration)	Jimmy started school <u>yesterday</u>. We'll <u>soon</u> be arriving at our destination. <u>Now</u> we can begin.
Adverbs of place	Come <u>here</u>, please. She ran <u>upstairs</u> to fetch her bags. The little boat drifted <u>ashore</u>.
Adverbs of manner	<u>Well</u> done, Susan. They <u>carefully</u> unwrapped the package. It rained <u>hard</u> last night.
Adverbs of degree	That's a <u>very</u> good story. This is <u>quite</u> funny. We <u>really</u> enjoyed your performance.

Adverbs can function in different ways, but there are two functions in particular that are worth mentioning here:

1. Conjunctive adverbs (such as however, furthermore, nevertheless and consequently) connect independent clauses (It was raining; however, sunshine was forecast for later in the day. . .).

2. Disjuncts are a type of adverb that indicate the writer's viewpoint or stance (Personally, I don't care whether you buy it or not. She was, surprisingly, on time!).

Adverbs are very flexible, in that they can typically be used in different positions in a sentence:

- <u>Quietly</u>, Marjorie tiptoed down the stairs.
- Marjorie <u>quietly</u> tiptoed down the stairs.
- Marjorie tiptoed <u>quietly</u> down the stairs.
- Marjorie tiptoed down the stairs <u>quietly</u>.

Many adverbs are formed by adding the –ly (or –ily/–ally) suffix to a related adjective (careless/carelessly; happy/happily; tragic/tragically). However, there are several other suffixes that can be used to form adverbs, notably –wards (backwards), –wise (clockwise) and –ways (sideways).

Some adverbs – known as 'flat adverbs' – take the same form as their adjectival equivalents (Come <u>quick</u>/the sun shone <u>bright</u> in the sky.) However, where a distinct –ly adverb form is available, many people consider flat adverbs to be non-standard.

Like adjectives, some adverbs have comparative and superlative forms. Some of these take the same form as their adjectival equivalents, so it's important to think carefully about the way they function in a sentence.

Teaching about adverbs

You could give pupils a passage and ask them how they might improve it by adding adverbs. The important thing is to emphasise that adverbs should be used appropriately and may not always be necessary.

The following passage might promote some interesting discussion as several of the verbs are highly descriptive in themselves, and may not necessarily be improved by the addition of adverbs. You could model this first, and then ask pupils to work on a similar passage, or consider how they might edit their own writing.

> The tiny coloured fish flicked in and out of the coral reef. Their scales glittered in the sunlight that was filtered through the water. The diver watched them as he swam towards the rocks. A large sea turtle emerged from the darkness of a small lagoon, and several small crabs nudged along the sea bed. . .

As adverbs are such a mobile word class, it's worth encouraging pupils to think about the effect of the position of an adverb in a sentence. One really effective way of doing this is by creating a 'human sentence'. Ask pupils to work in groups of five or six, and give them a sentence with each word printed separately on a sheet of A4 card. The sentence about Marjorie on the previous page would work well, but you can make up your own. You can include a full stop and a letter 'C' to represent a capital letter if you wish.

tiptoed	stairs	quietly	the	,	down	Marjorie

Ask each group to form a sentence by standing up and holding their card in front of them. (It helps if one pupil takes on the role of group coordinator.) The aim is to position the adverb in as many different places as possible within the sentence. As always with this type of activity, the discussion that it promotes is key, and you will need to tease out the impact of locating the adverb in each position – mid, front or end.

When introducing adverbs to younger children, you might use illustrations from a picture book to ask how a character is performing an action, e.g. How is the monster eating his marmalade sandwich? Greedily? Hungrily? Messily? Angrily? You could ask pupils to play 'guess the adverb' by acting out an action in a particular way (like a form of 'adverb charades'). Remember to log the best adverbs on the board or flip chart so that children can refer to them later or use them in their own writing.

WHEN MIGHT WE NEED TO USE ADVERBS IN WRITING?

Adverbs are so flexible, and modify so many different types of words, phrases and clauses, it's hard to write effectively without them.

What you need to know about prepositions

Prepositions are words that indicate the relationship between things, people or events, typically in terms of time or place. They usually come in front of a noun, pronoun or noun phrase. Prepositions introduce preposition phrases, which we'll look at in the chapter on phrases.

Time	Place
We arrived <u>after</u> lunch. The event will take place <u>during</u> the summer term. We'll leave <u>at</u> 5 o' clock.	She put the book <u>on</u> the table <u>in</u> the kitchen. Philip looked <u>behind</u> the sofa. Come and sit <u>next to</u> me.

Prepositions can also indicate relationships other than time or place. Consider the following prepositions, which indicate other aspects of the relationship between things, people or events:

- She bought the book <u>for</u> me.
- Would you like to come <u>with</u> me?
- He behaves just <u>like</u> my brother.
- She came to the party dressed <u>as</u> a monster.

Some prepositions consist of more than one word (in front of, because of, apart from, in spite of).

Sometimes you'll notice that a preposition doesn't come before a noun, pronoun or noun phrase and this is referred to as preposition stranding. Some people object to this, but it's quite acceptable, and sometimes there is no way of avoiding it. When there is an alternative, as in the sentences below, the second version is often considered more formal:

More informal	More formal
1. Who are you looking for?	2. For whom are you looking?
1. This is the coat I was looking for.	2. This is the coat for which I was looking.

Many prepositions can also function as adverbs or conjunctions, so it's important to look carefully at the way they are used in a sentence.

- Can you let me know <u>before</u> the end of the week? (preposition)
- I'll try to get there the day <u>before</u>. (adverb)
- She thought carefully <u>before</u> she replied. (conjunction)

Teaching about prepositions

When introducing prepositions to younger pupils, you could play a game such as *Where is my. . .?* You can use any item that's familiar to you and your children:

- Where is my apple?
- Where is my toy panda?
- Where is my key ring?

Play the game by hiding the object somewhere in the classroom and asking children to guess where it is. The rule is that they have to ask a question using a preposition:

- Is it <u>under</u> the table?
- Is it <u>on</u> your desk?
- Is it <u>next to</u> the paint pots?
- Is it <u>beneath</u> the. . .?

You could model this first by asking the questions yourself (having first asked another adult to hide the object), or you could provide a list of suitable prepositions on the learning wall to support pupils' choices.

You could give pupils a short passage with all the prepositions in a different colour and ask them to work out what 'job' these words are doing. It's best to focus on prepositions that indicate place or direction so that children can generalise from the activity before moving on to prepositions that fulfil other functions.

> Ginny woke up and peered **under** her bed. She couldn't see anything **in** the darkness so she ran **down** the stairs and slipped **into** the kitchen. She found a torch **on** the shelf **at** the back **of** the cupboard and tiptoed back **up** the stairs, carrying it carefully. . .

In any kind of procedural writing, it's important to be very precise with your use of prepositions. Consider the difference between 'Bake it <u>for</u> an hour' and 'Bake it <u>in</u> an hour'.

When writing instructions, help pupils to choose prepositions carefully to be clear and precise:

Turn left <u>after</u> the sign for the school.

Cross <u>over</u> the little bridge.

Continue slightly <u>to</u> the right.

Walk <u>up</u> the hill.

Our house is <u>on</u> the left.

You could give pupils a set of ambiguous instructions and ask them to try to follow them. Then they might rewrite them, using more precise and apt prepositions.

WHEN MIGHT WE NEED TO USE PREPOSITIONS IN WRITING?

It's hard to write without prepositions, especially when we want to show the precise relationship between where things are in relation to each other.

What you need to know about determiners

Determiners specify (or determine) a noun. It's helpful to know, for example, whether we are referring to <u>this</u> book, <u>Fred's</u> book, <u>the last</u> book or <u>every</u> book.

In noun phrases, determiners come before the noun, and typically before any adjectives that might also form part of the noun phrase. You can use more than one determiner in a noun phrase: <u>all the</u> best songs, <u>my first</u> boyfriend, <u>Jack's two</u> sisters.

Although some grammarians hold different views, it is generally accepted that determiners include the following:

- the definite and indefinite articles (the, a, an)
- quantifiers (there is a very long list of these, including all, both, some, each, every)
- numerals (two, the fifth, fifty-five)
- possessives (my, your, his, her, its, one's, our, your, their)
- demonstratives (this, these, that, those)
- interrogatives – whose, which, whichever, what, whatever
- the genitive – sometimes referred to as the possessive 's (<u>Sarah's</u> car, <u>my parents'</u> house).

Many of these words can also function as pronouns, so it's important to look carefully at the way they are used in a sentence. Determiners have to precede a noun to establish its reference or specificity; pronouns don't precede the noun because they are actually standing in for it.

Consider the difference between the following:

- <u>Which</u> book should I buy? (<u>which</u> functioning as a determiner)
- <u>Which</u> is the best book to buy? (<u>which</u> functioning as an interrogative pronoun)
- I couldn't decide <u>which</u> book to buy. (<u>which</u> functioning as a determiner)
- Don't you want <u>any</u> lunch today? (<u>any</u> functioning as a determiner)
- No thanks, I don't want <u>any</u>. (<u>any</u> functioning as a pronoun)
- This is my <u>second</u> attempt at swimming the Channel. (<u>second</u> functioning as a determiner)
- I made my first attempt to swim the Channel last year: this is my <u>second</u>. (<u>second</u> functioning as a pronoun)

Teaching about determiners

Younger pupils will need to be taught about the articles (the, a, an), which are a sub-set of determiners. They need to know when to use 'a' or 'an', particularly before a word beginning with the letter 'h'. (The general rule is that 'an' is used before a word that starts with a vowel sound, regardless of how it is spelt. If the 'h' is aspirated, it is treated as a consonant; if not, it is treated as a vowel.) You could give pupils a number of sentences and ask them what they notice about the use of 'a' and 'an' when it comes before a word that begins with the letter 'h'.

That was a horrible day!	There is not a hair on his head!
There is a horse in the field.	Can we stay in a hotel?
Let's climb up a hill.	It is an honour to receive this award.
I'll call you in an hour.	A hospital will be built here next year.
He'll give you an honest answer.	This old painting is an heirloom.

You might write a noun phrase on the board referenced by different determiners (a car/this car/my car/ Dad's car/every car) and ask pupils how the determiner affects the meaning in each. This could then be extended to sentences such as the following:

- I saw <u>a</u> white van driving fast down the road.
- I saw <u>the</u> white van driving fast down the road.
- I saw <u>Uncle Phil's</u> white van driving fast down the road.
- I saw <u>my</u> white van driving fast down the road.
- I saw <u>that</u> white van driving fast down the road.

This type of (seemingly simple) activity can promote rich discussion, requiring pupils to draw on active reading strategies such as inference, prediction and speculation.

You could give pupils a passage to edit. The passage below is written in a colloquial style, typical of speech, with some rather imprecise determiners. (In speech, we have the opportunity to clarify things for our listeners, and often refer to things that recipients can see or understand; in writing, we need to be more precise.) Ask pupils to identify five determiners in the passage that they would like to change and explain why.

I've just been to see <u>this</u> fantastic film about <u>a</u> boy who'd always loved swimming and wanted to be good enough to compete in <u>the</u> Olympics. He thought he had absolutely <u>no</u> chance of ever reaching <u>his</u> goal until <u>one</u> day he was spotted in <u>a</u> training session by <u>somebody's</u> coach who recognised <u>his</u> potential and agreed to give him <u>all</u> <u>these</u> tips to improve <u>his</u> performance. . .

WHEN MIGHT WE NEED TO USE DETERMINERS IN WRITING?

Determiners make a noun more specific, so we need to use them in most of our writing. Some nouns don't need to be referenced by a determiner (gerunds, for example, can function without one: <u>swimming</u> is good exercise/<u>talking</u> is not allowed), but most do, and careful choice can make writing more precise.

What you need to know about pronouns

Pronouns are words that stand in (like a substitute) for a noun or noun phrase. They help us to avoid unnecessary repetition and aid cohesion in writing.

- <u>Michael</u> looked out of the window. <u>He</u> was worried.
- Simi picked up <u>the heavy wooden box</u> and put <u>it</u> on the table.

There are different types of pronoun:

Personal pronouns refer to specific people or things. They have both subject and object forms:

	Subject personal pronouns	Object personal pronouns
singular	I, you, he, she, it	me, you, him, her, it
plural	we, you, they	us, you, them

Possessive pronouns indicate ownership (or possession). They are classed as either possessive pronouns or possessive determiners (sometimes referred to as possessive adjectives):

	Possessive pronouns	Possessive determiners
singular	mine, yours, his, hers	my, your, his, her, its
plural	ours, yours, theirs	our, your, their

'Its' can be used as a possessive determiner (the dog is wagging <u>its</u> tail), but not as a possessive pronoun.

Reflexive pronouns refer back to (or reflect) the subject of the clause. Notice the difference between *Tim helped himself* and *Tim helped him*.

	Reflexive pronouns
singular	myself, yourself, himself, herself, itself
plural	ourselves, yourselves, themselves

Interrogative pronouns are used to ask questions (interrogatives):

- who, whose, whom, what, whatever, which, whichever

Demonstrative pronouns are used to 'point to' things:

- this, that, these, those

Relative pronouns are used to introduce relative clauses:

- who, whom, whose, which, that

Reciprocal pronouns are used to indicate actions or feelings that are reciprocated:

- each other, one another

Indefinite pronouns refer to people or things in a less specific way:

- anybody, everyone, nothing, something

'One' can be used as a personal pronoun, a possessive pronoun (one's) and a reflexive pronoun (oneself). It is typically associated with more formal writing. (*If one finds oneself in an unfamiliar situation, one should not be alarmed.*)

Teaching about pronouns

One aspect of pronouns that pupils often find confusing is knowing when to use 'I' or 'me'. A good way to explore this is by using an investigative approach. Investigations can be effective because they enable pupils to work out rules and patterns for themselves. The approach works best when there is one clear rule which pupils can articulate so that they can generalise from the examples given. You'll need enough examples (at least 10–12) for the rule to be apparent.

Give pupils a collection of sentences that (correctly) use the grammatical pattern you want to explore – in this case it's 'I/me' – and ask them to work out the rule. (The answer is that you use 'I' when it's the subject of the sentence, and 'me' when it's the object of the sentence or when it comes after a preposition.) You might want to teach subject and object first, or you could use the activity to introduce this.

1. Sally and I decided to go swimming once a week.
2. The first prize was won by Ali and me as we had both achieved the top score.
3. Mum watched Kelly and me crossing the road.
4. It was a sunny day when I set out for the beach.
5. Last summer, my sister and I went on holiday together.
6. The runners sprinted after Katy and me.
7. 'Give it to me, please,' the teacher demanded.
8. My friends and I arranged to go for a pizza at the end of term.
9. That's the best present you've ever given me!
10. Even though it was raining, I still wanted to go for a walk.
11. Would you and Fran like to come with me and Simi?
12. I think you were before me in the queue.

Pronouns can be used to good effect in persuasive writing or formal argument. For example, we might address the reader directly (have you ever wondered why. . .) or include the reader in our point of view (we can't possibly believe that. . .). Give pupils a short piece of persuasive text and ask them to explore the way pronouns are used to engage the reader. You might ask them to highlight all the second-person (you) pronouns in one colour and all the first-person (I/we) pronouns in another.

As always, it's the discussion and the teasing out of key learning that makes this type of activity valid. A 'reading into writing' approach might then lead in to some modelled writing and shared composition before pupils have a go at writing their own persuasive pieces – ideally based on a different topic so that they can apply their learning independently.

Do you know how many black rhinos still exist? Did you realise that they are being hunted to extinction by poachers who sell their horns for profit? You might be wondering what we can do to help protect them. . . If we don't act now, this magnificent species will be lost forever. Will you give. . .

WHEN MIGHT WE NEED TO USE PRONOUNS IN WRITING?

We use pronouns to avoid unnecessary repetition in our writing, and to write more economically and cohesively. We'll look at pronouns again in the chapter on cohesion.

What you need to know about conjunctions

Conjunctions are words that join words, phrases and clauses. There are two types: coordinating conjunctions and subordinating conjunctions.

   Coordinating conjunctions (or coordinators) join words, phrases or clauses that are of equal status. The three main coordinating conjunctions are <u>and</u>, <u>but</u> and <u>or</u>.

Joining words and phrases	Joining clauses
My favourite meal is fish <u>and</u> chips.	We went to the park, <u>but</u> it started to rain.
Billy <u>and</u> Sandra are getting married next week.	Tom went shopping <u>and</u> bought a book.
You need to bring your swimming kit, a beach towel <u>and</u> some sun cream.	You can go swimming <u>or</u> you can go to the cinema.
We can have pasta <u>or</u> rice with our dinner.	Claire ran, cycled <u>and</u> swam every week.

Correlative coordinating conjunctions are pairs of coordinators which work together to join words, phrases or clauses. They include *either. . .or. . .*, *neither. . .nor. . .* and *not only. . .but also. . . .*

- We'll <u>either</u> go to Spain this year, <u>or</u> we'll stay at home.
- She has <u>neither</u> the good sense <u>nor</u> the <u>humility</u> to resign.
- The cafe <u>not only</u> serves great food, <u>but</u> it <u>also</u> has a fabulous view of the sea.

Subordinating conjunctions (or subordinators) join clauses that are not of equal status. One clause is dependent for its meaning on the other. Some common subordinating conjunctions are *because, if, although, as, since, so, unless* and *while*. Some subordinators consist of more than one word, such as *even if, in order that* and *as long as.*

- Come inside <u>before</u> you catch cold.
- <u>Although</u> I was tempted, I decided not to buy it.
- We wondered <u>whether</u> they had got lost.
- It was such a long time <u>since</u> she had played the piano in public.

Some conjunctions can function as other word classes, such as adverbs or prepositions, so it's important to look carefully at the way they are used in a sentence.

- Can you call me <u>after</u> lunch? (preposition)
- I'll try to get there the day <u>after</u>. (adverb)
- She went to bed <u>after</u> she had turned out the lights. (conjunction)

We'll look at how conjunctions are used to introduce clauses in the chapter on clauses.

Teaching about conjunctions

It makes sense to teach about conjunctions while teaching about coordination and subordination.

The sentence-combining approach, whereby pupils manipulate and experiment with grammatical structures, is known to be particularly effective. You might give pupils a number of clauses and a range of conjunctions and ask them to combine them in as many ways as possible to make different sentences.

Jimmy wanted to play football	because
	and
it started to rain	although
	while
Auntie Mary was coming to stay	if
	until
he needed to tidy his bedroom	as
	but
she came every August for two weeks	so
	since

You might give pupils a sentence with the same basic content and ask them to explain how the conjunction changes the meaning in each:

* Sam learnt to swim because he went to the pool with his friends.
* Sam learnt to swim and he went to the pool with his friends.
* Sam learnt to swim so he went to the pool with his friends.
* Sam learnt to swim when he went to the pool with his friends.

Developing writers often string multiple clauses together using 'and', as this reflects the speech patterns which are familiar to them. However, as children develop as writers, you'll want to encourage them to vary their use of conjunctions and to think about sentence structure. You may well pick this up as you respond to their writing, perhaps by asking them to edit a short section, by limiting the number of times they use 'and' or by offering two or three other conjunctions to be used as appropriate.

> On Saturday we went to the park and we played football and it started to rain and Uncle Pete said we would get soaked and we ran into the café and then Mum said we could each have an ice cream and. . .

WHEN MIGHT WE NEED TO USE CONJUNCTIONS IN WRITING?

Unless we are content to write in single-clause sentences, conjunctions are essential to writing, enabling us to extend ideas and express more complex relationships between ideas through coordination and subordination.

What you need to know about phrases and clauses

Some people like to define a phrase as a group of words that doesn't contain a verb, and a clause as a group of words that does contain a verb. This takes us only so far, until we encounter verb phrases, and verbless clauses, and discover that a noun phrase can consist of a single noun! Perhaps it's more helpful to consider both phrases and clauses as distinct grammatical units.

We might start with the sentence. Sentences are made up of clauses. They can consist of just one main clause. A single-clause sentence can consist of just a subject (a 'doer') and a finite verb:

- She shouted.
- I won!
- The dog barked.

Clauses are made up of phrases. Clauses also typically contain a subject and a verb, along with any other elements that might be necessary. Clauses can stand alone to form a single-clause sentence, or they can be subordinate to other clauses. We'll look at this later. There are different types of clauses:

- nominal clauses
- adverbial clauses
- relative clauses
- non-finite clauses.

We might think about phrases in terms of particular types of phrases:

- noun phrases
- preposition phrases
- adverb phrases
- adjective phrases.

We might say, then, that phrases and clauses are the building blocks of sentences.

In this chapter, we'll explore different types of phrases and clauses, including noun phrases, preposition phrases, adverbials (phrases and clauses), coordinated and subordinate clauses, relative clauses and non-finite clauses. We'll also look at subject and object.

You don't really need to know any more than this, so we won't cover adjective phrases, nor will we cover nominal clauses. However, if you're interested, they are described briefly here:

Adjective phrase: a group of words with an adjective as its 'head', typically modified by an adverb.
Lisa was <u>very happy</u> to hear the news. (adjective pre-modified by adverb)
The sea was <u>beautifully calm</u>. (adjective pre-modified by adverb)
These shoes aren't <u>big enough</u>. (adjective post-modified by adverb)
This ice cream is <u>really rather good</u>. (adjective pre-modified by two adverbs)

Nominal clause (or noun clause): a clause that functions as a noun or noun phrase. There is some disagreement amongst grammarians about noun clauses, which may also be referred to as content clauses.
<u>Learning to swim</u> is the hardest thing I've ever done.
<u>What she wanted</u> was a cup of strong, sweet tea.
I know <u>what I want</u>.

Teaching about phrases and clauses

What matters in terms of teaching and learning is that pupils are able to deploy phrases, clauses and sentences in their writing, varying them for effect with some degree of conscious control.

Once pupils are familiar with the types of phrases and clauses covered in this section, you can reinforce their application in writing by playing games such as 'composition cards' and 'clause consequences'.

For 'composition cards', pupils work in groups of three. Each group needs a set of composition cards (see below for examples), a mini whiteboard and a marker pen. The cards are shuffled face down, and pupils take it in turns to compose sentences as directed by the instructions on the cards. It's important to take the opportunity to share examples of really good sentences with the whole class, and explore what it is that makes them effective.

Compose a sentence which begins with a subordinate clause, e.g. <u>As I waited for my brother</u>, the bell rang.	Compose a sentence which begins with an adverbial phrase, e.g. <u>Later that evening</u>, we decided to go to the cinema.
Compose a sentence that consists of a single clause, modified by at least one preposition phrase, e.g. The teacher <u>in the red sports car</u> drove <u>into the car park</u>.	Compose a sentence that begins with an expanded noun phrase, e.g. <u>The tiny green caterpillar</u> munched its way through the cabbage leaves.
Compose a sentence with an embedded relative clause, e.g. Freddie, <u>who was the clumsiest boy in the class</u>, fell off his chair.	Compose a sentence which begins with at least two preposition phrases, e.g. <u>Near the old shed at the bottom of the garden</u>, my dad built us a tree house.
Compose a sentence with three coordinated clauses, e.g. Susan <u>plays the piano and sings, but she doesn't read music</u>.	Compose a sentence that begins with a non-finite clause using an –ing verb, e.g. <u>Walking slowly</u>, the old lady made her way home.

To make this more of a whole-class activity, you can play 'clause consequences'. Write a sentence on the board (it must contain at least one subordinate clause; for example, *As I scanned the horizon, I saw a small boat*) and ask pupils to choose from a set of cards, each containing an instruction. For example:

- change the subject of the sentence
- change the verb in the main clause
- move the subordinate clause.

You can ask pupils to compose and share orally, or they could write on mini whiteboards.

The whole point is to make this fun and creative. Little and often is best – it doesn't need a whole lesson. Be sure to ask pupils to log any really good sentences for later use.

What you need to know about noun phrases

A noun phrase is a group of words with a noun or pronoun as its 'head'. (Some grammarians recognise a single noun or pronoun as a noun phrase.)

Nouns can be pre-modified by adding words such as determiners, adjectives and adverbs in front of them:

- <u>castle</u> (head noun)
- <u>this</u> castle (add a determiner)
- this <u>old</u> castle (add an adjective)
- this <u>majestic</u> old castle (add another adjective)
- this <u>splendidly</u> majestic old castle (add an adverb).

Nouns can be post-modified by adding preposition phrases and relative clauses after them:

- this castle <u>on the cliff</u> (add a preposition phrase)
- this castle on the cliff <u>that overlooks the river</u> (add a relative clause).

Or they can be pre-modified *and* post-modified:

- this splendidly majestic old castle on the cliff that overlooks the river. . .

When we modify – or expand – a noun in this way, we create an expanded noun phrase.
Nouns can be modified in other ways too:

1. By other nouns – the <u>strawberry</u> pavlova, the <u>kitchen</u> window

2. By coordinated adjectives – that <u>pink and blue</u> shirt

3. By a non-finite relative clause (we'll look at this later in this section) – the cottage <u>overlooking the bay</u>, the trees <u>damaged by the storm</u>

A noun phrase can be part of a preposition phrase (down <u>the lonely country lane</u>, under <u>the apple tree laden with fruit</u>).

It's also possible for a noun phrase to be embedded in a longer noun phrase (the mischievous kitten with the black and white face). The head noun in this example is 'kitten'.

Teaching about noun phrases

You might share a menu consisting entirely of noun phrases like the one below. You could do this as a whole-class activity, by annotating the text on the board, or as a small-group activity. You could ask pupils why they think a text like a menu might make use of noun phrases in this way. Once you've established that noun phrases can condense a large amount of information into a limited space, you could ask pupils to think of their favourite meal and describe it using an expanded noun phrase. You could have a class vote on the one that sounds the most delicious.

> Prawn cocktail in a light seafood sauce
> Roast beef with Yorkshire pudding
> Fresh strawberries with Cornish clotted cream

You could explore how noun phrases are used in a range of advertisements. (You could ask pupils to look out for advertisements, for example in a newsagent's window, a local paper or a national magazine.) Again, it's important to establish why advertisements tend to use noun phrases in this way (whoever is placing the advertisement is paying for the space and so wants to pack as much information as possible into a limited space for maximum impact). You could ask pupils to make up their own advertisement using noun phrases, perhaps for a product they've made in technology or for a class cake sale.

For sale – nearly new bedroom furniture in excellent condition	Two-bedroom terraced cottage in highly desirable location
Two weeks in Corfu (including flights) for only £250 per person	Freshly baked bread from your local artisan bakery

You might explore the advertisement said to have been placed by Sir Ernest Shackleton to recruit men for his Antarctic expedition.

> Men wanted for hazardous journey. Small wages. Bitter cold. Long months of complete darkness. Constant danger. Safe return doubtful. Honour and recognition in case of success.

WHEN MIGHT WE NEED TO USE NOUN PHRASES IN WRITING?

Noun phrases help writers to condense a lot of information into a limited number of words, so they are particularly useful where space is at a premium, for example in advertisements. Expanded noun phrases can help us to add descriptive detail to our writing so they are particularly useful in descriptive writing and whenever precision and concision are necessary.

What you need to know about preposition phrases

Just as a noun acts as the head of a noun phrase, so a preposition acts as the head of a preposition phrase. A preposition phrase is introduced (or headed) by a preposition followed by a noun, noun phrase or pronoun.

- Would you pass this plate <u>to</u> Jack?
- I'll just put these bags <u>on</u> this table.
- They drove <u>over</u> the little stone bridge.
- I don't like to eat <u>before</u> swimming. (swimming is a gerund here, functioning as a noun)
- Is this <u>for</u> me?
- I don't really know what to think <u>about</u> this.

We've already met preposition phrases in the section on noun phrases, and we've seen how they can post-modify a noun to expand a noun phrase:

- The snuffling hedgehogs <u>under the rose bush</u>
- That old bike <u>in the tool shed</u>
- The pebbles <u>on the rocky shoreline</u>

Notice how several preposition phrases can be used incrementally to build a precise sense of location:

- <u>At the top</u> <u>of the staircase</u> <u>in the corner</u> <u>of the landing</u> sat. . .
- <u>Amongst the great boulders</u> <u>beneath the ocean waves</u> lurked. . .
- I knew that I always kept it <u>in the drawer</u> <u>of my desk</u> <u>in the study</u>. . .
- The thief was apprehended <u>at 1800 hours</u> <u>in the vicinity</u> <u>of the bike sheds</u>. . .

Preposition phrases can function adverbially in a sentence. Since prepositions are typically related to time and place, they can tell us more about when or where something happens, where someone or something is or how an action is performed. In other words, they can modify a verb.

The preposition phrases underlined in the sentences below all function adverbially and are therefore also referred to as adverbials.

- <u>After breakfast</u>, we'll go for a walk.
- Twenty-six lessons were observed <u>during the inspection</u>.
- The bells rang <u>at midnight</u>.
- <u>With some trepidation</u>, she walked to the end of the diving board.

Teaching about preposition phrases

Poetry offers rich opportunities to explore the powerful potential of these seemingly unobtrusive phrases. Look at the way they are used, for example, in Tennyson's 'The Charge of the Light Brigade' to create a sense of momentum, or the way they are used in 'The Highwayman' by Alfred Noyes to create a sense of impending doom for the lovers.

You could model a short 'preposition phrase poem', using preposition phrases to create a sense of intrigue before sealing the denouement with a single clause. Once pupils get the basic idea, you can ask them to write their own poems. If they need support, you could provide a bank of prepositions, or suggest a closing clause. Here are some examples:

In the darkness **Under** my bed My pencil case lurks.	**Against** the choppy waves **Underneath** the stars The little boat bobbed.
Below the gleaming moon **Beyond** the far horizon The wizard cast his spell.	**During** the school concert **With** a voice as clear as a bell I sang.

In science, model how to write up an experiment using preposition phrases for precision:

We poured a small amount of water <u>over the chalk</u> to see whether it would stay <u>on its surface</u> or soak <u>through it</u>. . .

WHEN MIGHT WE NEED TO USE PREPOSITION PHRASES IN WRITING?

Preposition phrases enable us to be precise about how, where and when things are in relation to each other. Since they can be used to expand noun phrases, they can help us to add detail to our writing, so they are particularly useful in descriptive writing, recounts, information and explanation writing.

What you need to know about adverbials

'Adverbial' is the word we use to describe a word, phrase or clause that functions adverbially. Single adverbs, adverb phrases, preposition phrases and subordinate clauses can all function as adverbials. Like adverbs, adverbials perform a wide range of functions.

They can tell us <u>when</u> something happened:

- She phoned us <u>yesterday morning</u>.
- <u>When we moved to this village</u>, we made lots of new friends.

They can tell us <u>where</u> something happened:

- You hit the ball <u>into those bushes</u>.
- We planted the roses <u>where the vegetable patch used to be</u>.

They can tell us <u>how</u> something happened:

- The teacher spoke <u>very firmly</u>.
- <u>With regret</u>, I must decline your offer.
- The sprinter ran <u>as fast as he could</u>.

They can tell us <u>why</u> something happened:

- I got into trouble <u>because of you</u>.
- I packed our bags last night <u>so that we wouldn't be late</u>.

Like adverbs, adverbials are very flexible, in that they can typically be used in different positions in a sentence.

They can be used in the end position:

- Sally slammed on her brakes <u>without warning</u>.
- Niall decided to go travelling <u>after university</u>.

They can also be fronted:

- <u>Without warning</u>, Sally slammed on her brakes.
- <u>After university</u>, Niall decided to go travelling.

Sometimes, they can go in mid-position:

- Sally – <u>without warning</u> – slammed on her breaks.
- Niall decided, <u>after university</u>, to go travelling.

A word of warning: sometimes we can inadvertently change the meaning by moving the adverbial. For example, did Niall not make his decision until he'd left university, or had he already made his decision before he completed his studies to go travelling once he'd finished his degree?

A comma is typically used after a fronted adverbial. We'll look at commas later in the chapter on punctuation.

Teaching about adverbials

One of the most important things you can teach your pupils about adverbials is the way they can be used in different positions in a sentence: this not only helps them to vary their sentences, but also enables them to shift the emphasis by foregrounding something they particularly want their reader to notice.

Consider the following two sentences:

* The snake slithered out of sight stealthily and without a sound.
* Stealthily and without a sound, the snake slithered out of sight.

By fronting the adverbial in the second sentence, the writer has foregrounded the action of the snake, making it seem more furtive and deliberate.

Now consider these two sentences:

* The giant squid loitered in the darkest depths of the ocean.
* In the darkest depths of the ocean, the giant squid loitered.

In the first sentence, the emphasis is on the giant squid, but by fronting the adverbial in the second sentence, the sense of place is foregrounded, creating an element of suspense and anticipation.

The main thing is to help pupils understand how they can shift the emphasis by moving the adverbial. It's not a question of one sentence being better than the other – it's about choice and conscious control, with the writer making deliberate choices to affect the reader's response.

Show pupils how to link ideas within and across sentences and paragraphs by using a range of conjunctive adverbials. If you do this through modelled and shared writing, you can articulate the reasons for your choices, helping pupils to understand which adverbials are the most appropriate in particular contexts and avoiding a formulaic approach. In particular, pupils need to understand that conjunctive adverbials join independent clauses within a sentence, as well as linking ideas across sentences and paragraphs.

* It was getting dark; <u>however</u>, they were determined to complete the walk.
* The campaign has raised awareness of road safety. <u>Nevertheless</u>, there is still much more to be done.

Conjunctive adverbials can be used to link ideas and information in different ways:

Adding	Illustrating	Reasoning	Contrasting	Summarising
Furthermore	For example	Consequently	In contrast	In conclusion
Moreover	For instance	Therefore	On the other	Overall
Also	In other words	Nevertheless	hand	Therefore
In addition	As shown by	As a result	However	Finally
As well as		Similarly	Alternatively	

WHEN MIGHT WE NEED TO USE ADVERBIALS IN WRITING?

Adverbials help to make writing more cohesive. They are so varied in form and function that they are necessary in most writing. For example, conjunctive adverbials – used appropriately – can signpost the reader through a balanced argument, a piece of evaluative writing in science, art or technology, or an explanation text in history or geography.

What you need to know about subject and object

Most clauses need, at the very least, a subject and a verb. We can say the following things about the subject of a clause:

- It is typically described as the 'doer' (or the agent) – the person or thing that performs the action of the verb. (Remember what we said in the first chapter: not all verbs indicate actions – they can denote states of being as well.)
- It is usually a noun or noun phrase, but can also be a pronoun or a nominal clause.
- In a statement clause, it typically comes before the verb and controls the form of the verb. This is what we mean by subject-verb agreement (or concord). A singular subject is followed by a verb in its singular form; a plural subject is followed by a verb in its plural form.

Example sentence	Subject
Jane wanted to learn to swim.	Jane: proper noun
They were training for the competition.	They: pronoun
The little brown dog wagged its tail.	The little brown dog: expanded noun phrase
Swimming is great exercise.	Swimming: gerund (verb functioning as a noun)
Learning to swim has helped me to keep fit.	Learning to swim: nominal clause
What she really wanted was a cup of tea.	What she really wanted: nominal clause

'It' and 'there' can function as 'dummy' or 'empty' subjects. They don't really carry any meaning, but simply fulfil the role of the subject.

- <u>It</u> is a lovely day.
- <u>There</u> are lots of reasons why the road should not be built.
- <u>There</u> is a noisy class next door.

Some clauses have an object as well as a subject. There are direct objects and indirect objects, and some clauses may have both. A clause cannot have an indirect object without a direct object.
   We can say the following things about an object:

- It is typically described as the recipient of the action of the verb, as it's affected by the action of the verb. (Remember that not all verbs indicate actions – they can denote states of being as well.)
- It is usually a noun or noun phrase, but can also be a pronoun or a nominal clause.
- It typically follows the verb.
- A direct object is more directly affected by the action of the verb than the indirect object.
- Indirect objects are usually people or animals.

Example sentence	Object
My cat scratched me.	Me: direct object
I took my dog for a walk.	My dog: direct object
Sally gave her friend a hug.	A hug: direct object Her friend: indirect object
The little brown dog wagged its tail.	Its tail: direct object
I handed my teacher the note.	The note: direct object My teacher: indirect object
Jane wanted to learn to swim.	No object

Teaching about subject and object

It's probably best to teach subject and object explicitly to the whole class by sharing some straightforward subject/verb/object (SVO) sentences and highlighting the subject and object in different colours.

That boy broke my pencil.	I found my pencil case.
Sally kicked the ball.	Jimmy bought five tickets.
My teacher sang a song.	We love swimming.

It's best to give a clear but simple explanation, perhaps identifying the subject as the 'doer' or the thing that 'does the doing' and the object as 'the thing that's done to' or 'the thing that's on the receiving end'.

What matters is that this knowledge is put to good use, for example in the following ways:

- teaching about the active and passive voice
- teaching when to use 'I' and 'me'
- teaching about subject-verb agreement
- teaching about Standard English and non-Standard forms of subject-verb agreement
- teaching how to vary the way we start sentences (for example, by not always using the basic subject/verb/object pattern).

You can draw on children's knowledge of nouns and noun phrases to explain that the head noun in a noun phrase needs to 'agree' with the verb when acting as the subject of a clause. Children often make mistakes with subject-verb agreement, especially when the subject consists of quite a lengthy expanded noun phrase, or when other phrases and clauses come between the subject and the verb.

- My <u>concerns</u> about your behaviour <u>are</u> as follows. . .
- The little black and white <u>dog</u> with the big, sad eyes <u>is</u> sitting on my doorstep.
- Those beautiful <u>flowers</u> in the bunch you gave me last week <u>have</u> lasted for ages.
- My auntie's <u>collection</u> of china plates <u>is</u> very valuable.

WHEN MIGHT WE NEED TO USE SUBJECT AND OBJECT IN WRITING?

It's important to understand about subject and object when forming the passive voice, and we'll look at this in the chapter on formality. It's also important when it comes to ensuring that subjects and verbs 'agree', particularly when using Standard English as opposed to non-Standard forms.

What you need to know about coordinated clauses

Coordinated clauses are clauses that have the same grammatical status as each other: each clause could stand alone as a main clause. Coordinated clauses are typically joined by a coordinating conjunction.

Many grammarians refer to sentences consisting of two or more coordinated clauses as compound sentences.

Sometimes, coordinated clauses share the same subject:

- Ginny tripped and fell. (Ginny tripped and <u>Ginny</u> fell.)
- We turned the corner and saw the most amazing sight! (We turned the corner and <u>we</u> saw the most amazing sight!)
- I wanted to improve my Spanish, but didn't know where to start. (I wanted to improve my Spanish, but <u>I</u> didn't know where to start.)
- Should I stay or go? (Should I stay or <u>should I</u> go?)

It's usual to omit the subject in the second clause, as this can support cohesion and concision. However, there may be times when you decide to repeat the subject, as in the last bracketed example above where the repetition of 'should I' reinforces the sense of the speaker's dilemma.

Sometimes, coordinated clauses may have different subjects:

- The dogs barked and the sheep bleated.
- My friends weren't keen, but I really wanted to go to the party.
- I can drive over to you or you could come here. . .

Notice that it's usual to put a comma before 'but' when it introduces a clause.

Sentences can contain multiple coordination – in other words, they can contain more than two coordinated clauses:

- He wanted to see a film <u>and</u> then go for a meal, <u>but</u> it was getting late <u>and</u> I wanted an early night.
- Then I'll huff <u>and</u> I'll puff, <u>and</u> I'll blow your house down. Well, he huffed <u>and</u> he puffed, <u>and</u> he puffed <u>and</u> he huffed, <u>but</u> he still could not blow the house down.

A 'list' of coordinated clauses can be separated by commas. Notice how a coordinating conjunction is used to join the last two clauses.

- He ran down the road, turned the corner, and disappeared out of sight.

(It's important to note that this is not the same as a comma splice, which should never be used to separate sentences. We'll return to this in the chapter on punctuation.)

Although their prime function is to join clauses, coordinating conjunctions can be used for stylistic effect to start a sentence, although this is generally less typical in more formal writing.

- He couldn't contemplate stealing from his best friend. Or could he?
- Horace locked the drawer and replaced the key. But he couldn't resist leaving the door slightly ajar. . .

Teaching about coordinated clauses

Developing writers tend to string coordinated clauses together, typically joined by 'and'. We do the same in informal speech, so it's not surprising that young children reflect this in their writing. Coordination has its place in more mature writing too though, and shouldn't be regarded as in any way inferior to subordination. You might consider the impact of the coordinated clauses in the following:

- The wind howled and the thunder crashed and the rain poured down. The old house closed its shutters to the storm.
- He begged and entreated and wept, but to no avail. The door clicked gently shut behind her.
- They clapped their hands and wriggled in their seats and chuckled in delight. The day of the twins' birthday party had arrived.

You could model similar sentences and tease out the way the repeated coordination creates a sense of anticipation by slowing the pace of the writing. Then ask pupils to write two similar sentences using the same grammatical structure:

Sentence 1
clause + *and* + clause + *and* + clause (+ optional *but* + clause).
Sentence 2
single clause

This 'creative imitation' approach enables pupils to 'try a sentence on for size' – adapting and importing the pattern into their own writing.

You could give pupils three or four short, single-clause sentences and ask them to rewrite them as one sentence, using different coordinating conjunctions. You could give these to pupils on cards so that they can manipulate them easily, perhaps in pairs or small groups. It's important to tease out the different uses of the coordinators, for example to give additional information (*and*), or to provide contrasting (*but*) or alternative (*or*) information.

and	or	but

Clara loves peanut butter.	She hates strawberry jam.
They could go for a bike ride.	They could go swimming.
We'll stop for lunch.	We'll finish this later.

WHEN MIGHT WE NEED TO USE COORDINATED CLAUSES IN WRITING?

As well as providing a sense of balance in writing, coordinated clauses can be used stylistically to slow the pace and create a sense of anticipation through deferred gratification. For this reason, they can be employed to particularly good effect in any writing where you want to build an atmosphere of suspense. They can be particularly effective when juxtaposed with a short, single-clause sentence.

What you need to know about subordinate clauses

A subordinate clause is dependent for its meaning on a main (or independent) clause. For this reason, subordinate clauses are sometimes referred to as dependent clauses. Subordinate clauses are typically introduced by a subordinating conjunction, although they can also be introduced by a non-finite verb – more on these later.

A subordinate clause can't stand on its own as a sentence. The following subordinate clauses simply don't make sense on their own:

| because it was raining |
| until it was dark |
| if it is sunny tomorrow |

However, if we add a main clause, they make perfect sense:

| We stayed indoors because it was raining. |
| We played in the garden until it was dark. |
| If it is sunny tomorrow, we'll go to the beach. |

Many grammarians refer to sentences containing one or more subordinate clauses as complex sentences. Although this is an established grammatical term, it can give the impression that the meaning conveyed by the sentence is complex, which is not necessarily the case. Similarly, a sentence that contains a single clause is often referred to as a simple sentence, even though its structure and the ideas it conveys may not be simple at all. Consider the following:

| I went to bed because I was tired. | 'Complex' sentence containing a subordinate clause (because I was tired). |
| The headteacher carefully reversed his little red sports car into the last space in the school car park. | 'Simple' sentence containing a single clause (The headteacher reversed his car). |

For this reason, many people prefer to refer to single-clause and multi-clause sentences.

Subordinate clauses can typically appear in different positions in a sentence.

1. They can go at the end of a main clause:
   The teacher decided to finish the session early because it was late.

2. They can go at the front of a main clause:
   Because it was late, the teacher decided to finish the session early.

3. They can be embedded in the middle of a main clause:
   The teacher, because it was late, decided to finish the session early.

Notice that a single comma is used to buffer the fronted clause from the main clause, and a pair of commas is used to buffer the embedded clause from the main clause.

Teaching about subordinate clauses

You can introduce subordination to younger pupils by modelling it in spoken language whenever you want them to expand their answers and explanations. Children can be supported and prompted to do this by using oral sentence starter cards or by displaying and referring to key subordinators on the learning wall.

I like Holly's picture <u>because</u>. . .
I enjoyed this book <u>because</u>. . .
I thought the baby owls were lonely <u>because</u>. . .

Show pupils how to use subordination through modelled and shared writing, articulating the reasons for your choices, and re-reading to check for meaning and effect. You can demonstrate how layers of meaning can be built up in a single sentence:

* The cyclist won the race <u>after his main opponent was disqualified</u> <u>when he broke the takeover rules,</u> <u>forcing another cyclist off the track.</u>
* The swimmers raced on, <u>paying no heed to the rough waves,</u> <u>until they reached the shore</u>.
* We can't always predict <u>when an earthquake will happen,</u> <u>even in countries that are renowned for them,</u> <u>which makes it impossible</u> to be completely prepared.

Use an investigative approach to show pupils how commas are used to buffer fronted subordinate clauses. (This is best done once pupils have some understanding of subordinate clauses.) Give pupils a number of sentences and ask them why they think commas are used in only some of the sentences. Remember that you'll need enough examples for the rule to be apparent so that pupils can generalise from the examples given. If you prefer, you could give them sentences that contain embedded subordinate clauses in mid-position too, or you could add these in later.

After he had finished his book, Robin turned out the light.	She forgot to pick up her keys before she slammed the door.
I will clear away the dishes if you help me.	We might go for a walk when it stops raining.
Once he started college, Philip made lots of new friends.	Sini looked in the shop window while she waited for her brother.
Although the puppy had been trained, it still barked loudly at the postman.	Even though it was late, they decided to walk home from the cinema.

WHEN MIGHT WE NEED TO USE SUBORDINATE CLAUSES IN WRITING?

Subordination enables writers to express more complex ideas by building layers of meaning. It's essential in most writing across all subjects.

What you need to know about relative clauses

A relative clause is a type of subordinate clause that post-modifies a noun as part of an expanded noun phrase. It is introduced by a relative pronoun (who, whom, whose, which, that).

- This is the book <u>that I bought</u>.
- The train, <u>which was crowded</u>, pulled out of the station.
- I went to see my best friend, <u>who I had known since I was five</u>.
- My best friend, <u>whose parents live in Scotland</u>, has just moved to Cornwall.

The relative adverbs *when*, *where* and *why* can also introduce a relative clause:

- That was the moment <u>when I knew I loved her.</u>
- This is the house <u>where I grew up</u>.
- My workaholic lifestyle was the reason <u>why she left</u>.

(You need to remember that *where*, *when* and *that* can also function as subordinating conjunctions to introduce a straightforward subordinate clause – be careful not to confuse these with relative clauses.)

Sometimes the relative pronoun is omitted altogether: this is also referred to as a 'zero' relative pronoun.

- This is the book <u>I bought</u>.
- Is that the song <u>you like</u>?
- That was the moment <u>I knew I loved her</u>.

Relative clauses can be defining (restrictive) or non-defining (non-restrictive).

Defining (restrictive) relative clauses define the noun they follow:

- My friend who lives in London is selling her house.

The relative clause (*who lives in London*) refers to my specific friend who lives in London rather than any of my other friends who live elsewhere.

Non-defining (non-restrictive) relative clauses simply provide additional information that is not essential to the meaning.

- My friend, who lives in London, is selling her house.

In this sentence, the fact that my friend lives in London is interesting, but non-essential information.

Notice how a pair of commas (brackets or dashes could be used instead) is used to mark the non-defining relative clause, as it provides information that could be removed from the sentence without changing its meaning. (The relative pronoun 'that' tends not to be used to introduce a non-defining relative clause.)

Sentential relative clauses refer to a preceding clause or sentence. They are introduced by the relative pronoun 'which'.

- She decided to train to be a hairdresser, <u>which was a really good idea</u>.
- After we'd visited Australia, we travelled on to New Zealand – <u>which was absolutely brilliant</u>!

Teaching about relative clauses

An effective way to teach about relative clauses is to use the sentence-combining approach. Give pupils two or three short sentences and ask them to combine them into one sentence, using a relative clause. They should try to retain as much of the information as possible.

Jane has a sister.	Her sister lives in Spain.	She is going to visit her sister next month.
Julius Caesar was a Roman general.	The Romans invaded Britain in 55 BC.	Julius Caesar led the Roman army.
Plants grow in soil.	A plant's roots anchor it in the soil.	A plant's roots draw water and nutrients from the soil to feed the plant.

Of course, there may be more than one way of doing this, which would provide fruitful class discussion. Here are some possibilities:

1. Jane is going to visit her sister, who lives in Spain, next month.
2. The Roman army, which invaded Britain in 55 BC, was led by Julius Caesar.
3. A plant's roots, which help to anchor it, draw water and nutrients from the soil to feed it.

You could use an investigative approach to help pupils understand the difference between defining and non-defining relative clauses. Give them a number of sentences and ask them to work out the difference in meaning between those that have commas and those that don't. Remember that you'll need enough examples for the rule to be apparent so that pupils can generalise from the examples given.

The boys who misbehave in class are in trouble with the headteacher.	The boys, who misbehave in class, are in trouble with the headteacher.
Dog owners who walk their dogs every day are usually fit and healthy.	Dog owners, who walk their dogs every day, are usually fit and healthy.
The villagers who organised the protest were successful in preventing the development.	The villagers, who organised the protest, were successful in preventing the development.
My sister who plays the violin in an orchestra is twenty-five next week.	My sister, who plays the violin in an orchestra, is twenty-five next week.
Children who eat too many sweets have bad teeth.	Children, who eat too many sweets, have bad teeth.
Girls who work hard do well at school.	Girls, who work hard, do well at school.

WHEN MIGHT WE NEED TO USE RELATIVE CLAUSES IN WRITING?

Relative clauses can be used to expand noun phrases. They help writers to condense information into a limited number of words, and to write with economy and precision. They are particularly useful in information and explanation texts where information needs to be presented clearly and succinctly.

What you need to know about non-finite clauses

A non-finite clause is a type of subordinate clause that takes a non-finite verb. Unlike a finite verb, a non-finite verb doesn't reveal its tense. For this reason, it is sometimes referred to as a non-tensed verb form.

Non-finite verbs are formed in three ways:

1. The –ed form (sometimes called the past participle or the –ed participle)

2. The –ing form (sometimes called the present participle or the –ing participle)

3. The infinitive form (the base form of the verb preceded by 'to')

A non-finite clause using the –ed form	<u>Supported by the cheers of the crowd</u>, the team went on to win the match.
A non-finite clause using the –ing form	<u>Struggling to complete the race</u>, the runner was on the point of giving up.
A non-finite clause using the infinitive form	<u>To win the gold medal</u>, the athlete had trained every day.

We've already seen how subordinate clauses depend for their meaning on the main clause. However, non-finite clauses make the reader work even harder: because they don't indicate tense, the reader has to look to the main clause to find out the who/what and when – in other words, the subject and the tense of the verb.

Non-finite clause	Main clause
Supported by the cheers of the crowd,	the team went on to win the match.
Struggling to complete the race,	the runner was on the point of giving up.
To win the gold medal,	the athlete had trained every day.

Non-finite clauses are highly mobile, and can be moved to different positions in a sentence for effect and emphasis.

*   <u>Sobbing quietly</u>, the small child searched in vain for its mother.
*   The small child, <u>sobbing quietly</u>, searched in vain for its mother.
*   The small child searched in vain for its mother, <u>sobbing quietly</u>.

Teaching about non-finite clauses

You could use a 'sentence-building' approach to explore the effect of placing a non-finite clause in different positions in a sentence.

Put pupils into groups of five or six and give them a set of cards like the ones below. You'll notice that these include adverbials (*after a strenuous day/in their basket*), a subject (*the tiny kittens*) and a verb (*curled up*) as well as a non-finite clause (*purring contentedly*). You can make up your own if you prefer. You might wish to include a full stop, several commas and a letter 'C' to represent a capital letter.

the tiny kittens
after a strenuous day
in their basket
purring contentedly
curled up

(They need to be printed on large strips of card so pupils can hold them in front of them to form a 'human sentence' so that the rest of the class can read the sentences other groups have formed.)

Ask each group to share out their cards. The aim is to position the non-finite clause in as many different places as possible within the sentence. (This is best done if they stand up and hold their card in front of them, although it could also be done as a table activity. It also helps if one pupil takes on the role of group coordinator.)

Ask several groups to present their different versions to the class and discuss the shifts in emphasis and meaning. As always with this type of activity, the discussion it promotes is key, and you will need to tease out the impact of the different positions of the non-finite clause:

* <u>Purring contentedly</u>, the tiny kittens curled up in their basket after a strenuous day.
* The tiny kittens, <u>purring contentedly</u> after a strenuous day, curled up in their basket.
* After a strenuous day in their basket, the tiny kittens curled up – <u>purring contentedly</u>.

You might then ask pupils what punctuation they need, apart from a capital letter and full stop (this would be a good opportunity to distribute your comma cards).

There should be plenty of opportunities to comment on the way writers use non-finite clauses in fiction and non-fiction texts, and this can also be modelled as a focus for shared writing. Once pupils are familiar with non-finite clauses, you can remind them to vary their sentence structure in their writing by thinking about when it might be appropriate to start a sentence with a non-finite clause. If you haven't introduced the terminology (it's not required by the national curriculum), you could simply ask them to start with an –ing or an –ed verb.

WHEN MIGHT WE NEED TO USE NON-FINITE CLAUSES IN WRITING?

Non-finite clauses are used in a range of writing, from the very formal to the informal and across a range of genres. Because they are highly mobile, they can add variety to sentence structure, and can help to emphasise or foreground particular elements in descriptive or narrative writing.

What you need to know about sentence forms and functions

Sentences can perform different functions: they can provide or seek information, give instructions, issue commands and much more. We can usually identify the function of a sentence from the form of its main clause. We'll look at this more closely over the next few pages.

There are four clause types that indicate a sentence's function:

1. **Declaratives** typically give information. We'll refer to these as **statements**.

    - I love cats.
    - Every year, Shirley went on holiday to Spain.
    - Although it was raining, Kamil decided to go running.

2. **Interrogatives** typically ask for information or some kind of reply or response. We'll refer to these as **questions**.

    - Would you like an ice cream?
    - Where are my keys?
    - Shall we go swimming today?

3. **Imperatives** typically tell you to do (or not to do) something. We'll refer to these as **commands**, although many grammarians prefer the term **directives**, of which commands are a particular sub-set.

    - Sit down!
    - Don't forget to turn the light off.
    - Bake in a hot oven for half an hour.

4. **Exclamatives** typically express strong emotion. We'll refer to these as **exclamations**.

    - What a fantastic day that was!
    - How kind you are!
    - How I wish you would turn that music down!

Teaching about sentence forms and functions

Sentences with different forms are taught at Key Stage 1, including the terminology *statement*, *question*, *exclamation* and *command*. At Key Stage 2, pupils will build on this knowledge, deploying sentence forms appropriately in their writing and making more conscious choices about their use.

In speech, it's usually fairly clear from our intonation whether we're asking a question, issuing an instruction or stating some information. However, it's important to acknowledge that – especially in speech – some sentence forms can function in ways that don't seem to correspond with their form. For example, the following sentences use an interrogative form and yet they really appear to be masquerading as polite commands:

- Please would you pass the pepper?
- Will you shut the window?

In writing, we need to choose the correct – or sometimes the most appropriate – punctuation to demarcate our sentences. A writer's choice of punctuation doesn't change the form of a sentence. For example, an exclamation mark can demarcate a statement or a command, but this doesn't make them exclamations. Similarly, a statement demarcated by a question mark may seem to function as a question, but its form remains that of a statement.

Your pupils need to know about sentences with different forms, and they need to understand that these sentences have different functions in writing. Most importantly of all, they need to be able to deploy them to good effect in their own writing, making the conscious choices that good writers make when they have different options at their disposal.

Unless we're writing a recipe or an instruction manual, we're likely to find that statements tend to be the 'default' model in most writing. For this reason, when questions, commands or exclamations are used in particularly interesting or effective ways, it's worth taking the time to explore their use and impact with pupils.

In the pages that follow, we'll look at each sentence form in more detail.

What you need to know about statements

Statements fall into the category of declaratives. Their function is primarily to give information, which they do in a range of ways, such as describing, commenting and explaining. They can also answer questions.

The main thing to remember about the form of a statement is that the subject almost always comes before the verb. The structure looks like this:

Subject + *verb* + any other elements

Terry *swims* every week at the local pool.

The ducks, geese and chickens *lived* on the farm.

Every Saturday, **I** *go* to the library in town.

The following passage is composed entirely of statements.

Rashida was looking forward to her birthday. Her mum had promised to arrange a party for her friends, and Rashida had enjoyed writing the invitations. However, when the day came, Rashida woke with a terrible headache. She was shivery and felt sick. 'You might be coming down with the 'flu,' said Mum. 'I'd better ring your friends and tell them that the party will have to be postponed.'

Teaching about statements

We use statements all the time, when we speak and when we write. You'll need to help your pupils to recognise the statement form (as distinct from other sentence forms) and to know the terminology. It can be particularly tricky when a statement starts with a wh– word (usually associated with questions) such as *What I really wanted was a chocolate ice cream.*

Ask pupils to tell each other five things that they know or believe to be true. They might say something like this:

- My cat's name is Jessie.
- I have a little brother.
- My birthday is in July.
- We cycle to school every day.
- Our class learnt about plants in science.

Take feedback, choosing two or three suitable examples to write up on the board. Show pupils how each sentence follows the same pattern: each sentence has a verb, and a person or thing that is 'doing the action in the verb' which comes before it. (It might be helpful to write these in two different colours to support pupils' understanding.) You'll need to pay particular attention to the verbs *be, do* and *have* as children won't necessarily see these as 'actions'. (This is why it's not particularly helpful to describe verbs as 'doing' words.)

To consolidate this, give pupils a set of statements on cards and ask them to underline or highlight the verb in one colour and the person or thing that is 'doing the action' in a different colour. Tease out what they notice about the order – which comes first? Alternatively, you could give them a set of words on cards and ask them to arrange them into a statement. (If children do put them in the wrong order, you can discuss any errors or misconceptions with the class.)

You could give pupils a passage like the one below which, apart from one question, consists entirely of statements. Ask them to find the sentence that isn't a statement.

Mia wanted to play in the park. She liked the swings and the slide. She liked the big roundabout. Best of all, she liked the big, green climbing frame. 'Could we go to the park tomorrow?' Mia asked her dad. 'We could take a picnic.'

Once pupils are confident with this, show them how they can turn the question into a statement by reversing the order of the modal verb and the 'doer' (subject) like this:

We could go to the park tomorrow.

If pupils need a little more support, you could ask them to rearrange given words on cards into a statement and then change it into a question:

swimming	?	go	.	we	can

WHEN MIGHT WE NEED TO USE STATEMENTS IN WRITING?

We tend to use statements in most of our writing, apart from sets of instructions, where they may not be required at all. Recounts (such as writing up a science experiment), information, explanation and description all rely on statements. Narrative (such as story writing) also relies heavily on statements, although there is likely to be some use of questions, commands and exclamations, especially in any dialogue used.

What you need to know about questions

Questions fall into the category of interrogatives. When we ask a question, we usually expect some kind of response, such as an answer, that provides the information required.

Sometimes we ask questions to which we already know the answer – teachers do this all the time – and sometimes we ask rhetorical questions which don't require an answer at all, but are used for rhetorical effect. (*Who do you think you're talking to? Why didn't he check the route before setting off?*)

Questions can be formed in different ways.

1. They can start with a wh– word: what, which, who, whom, whose, where, why, when – and how. This group of words includes interrogative pronouns (who, whom, whose, what, which) as well as words that function as other word classes. With the exception of *how*, they all begin with wh–, which makes them easy to remember.

Who did that?

Which song do you like best?

When are you going on holiday?

Whose pencil case is this?

2. They can start with an auxiliary verb (do, have, be) or a modal verb (can, could, shall, should, will, would, may, might, must). When a question starts in this way, the subject ('doer') and verb are inverted: in other words, the subject comes <u>after</u> the auxiliary/modal verb.

Is Sheila coming tonight?

Could you manage another piece of cake?

Shall we look at this together?

Are you the pianist?

3. They can use a question tag, which mirrors the subject and auxiliary verb of the declarative clause that precedes it. However, because these sentences are technically formed of a statement plus a question, some grammarians don't class them as true questions. They are generally used in speech and in more informal situations.

She's definitely coming tonight, *isn't she*?

Margaret had promised to help, *hadn't she*?

I'm the best swimmer, *aren't I*?

In writing, questions are demarcated by a question mark. However, it's not possible to turn a statement into a question simply by using a question mark in writing or by using a rising intonation in speech. (*Katie has a new car?*) Even though the sentence seems to function as a question, its form remains that of a statement.

Teaching about questions

Once you've taught your pupils about statements, it makes sense to show them how to turn a statement into a question by inverting (or reversing) the order of the subject and verb: *I can swim* becomes *Can I swim? Ali is coming to my party* becomes *Is Ali coming to my party?* It's best to model this initially, so that you can show pupils how to invert the subject and the verb, and talk them through the process.

You might ask pupils to generate questions by working in pairs to interview each other. They might do this as a role play, with one pupil interviewing a character from a story the class has read together, a well-known person from history or a current celebrity. (You might explore the difference between open and closed questions: closed questions require a yes/no response, and are quite different from open questions that require more open and extended responses.)

Log some of their questions on the board and tease out the types of questions they've used. You could display these on a learning wall under different headings, e.g. wh– questions; questions that use an auxiliary verb (do, have, be); questions that use a modal verb. With younger pupils, you can do this without using the terminology (even though pupils may not be taught about modal verbs until year 5, younger pupils are more than likely to be familiar with their use).

You could give pupils a statement and ask them to suggest the question that might have prompted it.

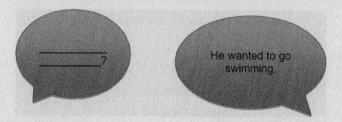

_____?

He wanted to go swimming.

Alternatively, you could give them a picture and ask them to generate a number of wh– questions that they would like to ask about it. You could put pupils in teams, and challenge each team to think of the most questions.

Another approach is to look at the lead paragraph of a newspaper report and ask a who, what, where, when, why and how question to see how successful it is as a lead paragraph. Here's an example:

> Two men were rescued from the sea yesterday when their boat started to sink off the coast in Cornwall.

WHEN MIGHT WE NEED TO USE QUESTIONS IN WRITING?

Questions allow a writer to directly address the reader so they are often used in writing that aims to persuade or influence. Older pupils can be taught how to use rhetorical questions in persuasive writing and formal argument. Younger writers are likely to use questions in narrative, especially in dialogue. In information texts, they might choose to frame sub-headings or fact boxes as questions, with information providing the answers in the sections that follow.

What you need to know about commands

Commands fall into the category of directives. Directives fulfil a broad range of functions: they can be used to give instructions (*Put on your life jacket*), make a polite request (*Please sit here*), issue an invitation (*Do come to my party*), offer advice (*Think carefully before answering*), wish somebody well (*Have a good day*) and give warnings (*Watch out!*). This is why many grammarians tend to regard commands as a sub-set of directives.

Commands use the imperative form, which uses the base form of the verb.

Look over there.

Follow me.

When the music stops, *stand* absolutely still.

Sarah, *turn* that music down.

Stop writing and *put* down your pens.

Imperatives rarely include the subject (the subject – *you* – is implied).

(You) look over there.

(You) follow me.

Negative commands are formed by *do not/don't*.

Don't look.

Do not follow me.

Let can also be used as an imperative, but it works in a slightly different way to other verbs. Notice how the negative can be formed in different ways:

Let's go swimming.

Let us pray.

Don't let's quarrel.

Let's not quarrel.

Teaching about commands

Teachers often call these 'bossy verbs', but there's no reason why you shouldn't share the appropriate grammatical terminology. It might help to tell them the meaning of the word 'imperative' which, as an adjective, means peremptory, commanding or bossy.

Pupils are likely to be familiar with commands, but they need to understand how to use the base form of the verb. It's worth discussing why this might be: commands need to be clear and to the point, with no room for ambiguity.

> *Stop!*
> When you reach the end of the road, *turn* left.
> *Bake* in a hot oven.

It's worth exploring the difference between a statement that functions as a polite request (*I'd like you to sit down now*) and a command that uses the imperative (*Sit down now*). You might give pupils a number of sentences and ask them which one is a command. The imperative verb may not necessarily appear right at the start of the sentence, and may therefore be more difficult to spot (*Sally, please put that down*).

As with other sentence forms, it's possible to give pupils a statement or a question and ask them to rewrite it as a command. However, unlike statements and questions, which can easily be transposed using the same set of words, commands need a little more reworking.

- Ravi did work hard at school. (statement)
- Did Ravi work hard at school? (question)
- Work hard at school, Ravi. (command)

You might ask pupils to collect examples of any commands they see around the school or in the local area:

> Do not run in the corridor.
> Put your library books back on the shelves.
> Please queue here.

WHEN MIGHT WE NEED TO USE COMMANDS IN WRITING?

Instructions use the imperative form, so any set of instructions (including recipes) requires this sentence form. Commands might also feature in dialogue in a narrative, or in a director's notes on a play script.

What you need to know about exclamations

Exclamations fall into the category of exclamatives. They can express strong emotion, such as surprise, anger, delight – or even puzzlement. They can be single words (also known as interjections), phrases or sentences:

Wow! Gosh! Ouch!

How funny! What an amazing day!

How brave you are! What a brilliant story that was!

Exclamations that are *sentences* have the following forms:

What + *noun/noun phrase* + **subject** + <u>verb</u> + any other elements

What *a lovely day* **we** <u>had</u> yesterday!

How + *adjective* + **subject** + <u>verb</u> + any other elements

How *cosy* **the little cottage** <u>looked</u> in the forest!

How + *adverb* + **subject** + <u>verb</u> + any other elements

How *beautifully* **Sara** <u>sang</u> in the concert!

How + *clause* (subject/verb) + any other elements

How *I wish* we could go home!

Exclamations are usually demarcated by an exclamation mark (!). Other forms of sentence (such as commands or statements) can also be demarcated by an exclamation mark: writers tend to do this when they want to add emotive force or emphasis, or to show that a character is shouting:

'Look out!' yelled Tommy.

There was a terrific thunderstorm and we got drenched!

However, the use of an exclamation mark doesn't make these sentences exclamations: they are still commands or statements.

Teaching about exclamations

It's important to remember that the national curriculum specifies sentences with different forms, so pupils need to be aware of the differences between one-word interjections, exclamative phrases and sentences.

Exclamations tend to be less widely used than the other sentence forms, so you can't necessarily rely on pupils being exposed to them in everyday situations. You'll often find exclamations in traditional tales and poems such as *Little Red Riding Hood* and *The Owl and the Pussycat*.

- What big teeth you have, Grandma!
- How charmingly sweet you sing!

You can draw attention to these through your work on storytelling and poetry performance so that pupils absorb the patterns and rhythms of this sentence form. Pupils can make up their own exclamations by substituting one or two words from a given example: *What big teeth you have, Grandma!* might become *What long hair you have, Sally!* or *What great stories he tells!* A single sentence can provide pupils with a model which they can then adapt and use in their own writing, whenever appropriate.

You could use a more 'hands-on' inductive approach by giving pupils a selection of sentences on cards. You might restrict these to questions and exclamations that start with 'what' or 'how', depending on how much your pupils already know about sentence forms. It's best to leave off the question marks and exclamations marks, but do tell your class that you've done this! Ask pupils to sort the cards into questions and exclamations. (Ideally, this is done in pairs or threes so that they can talk about the reasons for their choices.) It might help to provide a clue, e.g. In the questions, the word 'what' is followed by a verb; in the exclamations, it is followed by a noun or a noun phrase.

What is your teacher's name	What a sad story this is
What fun that was	What is your favourite colour
What do you like to eat	What silly jokes he tells

Once children have been taught the main sentence forms (statements, questions, commands, exclamations), show them how to take a straightforward statement or question and rewrite it as an exclamation, using as many of the same words as possible, e.g.

- This is a funny story.
- Is this a funny story?
- What a funny story this is!

WHEN MIGHT WE NEED TO USE EXCLAMATIONS IN WRITING?

Exclamations will probably be used quite sparingly, and are more typically used in speech. In writing, they might be used in dialogue in either narrative or play scripts, or when the writer wants to express a strongly held view or emotion.

Cohesion: making connections within and across a text

What you need to know about cohesion

Cohesion relates to the way a text is woven together. Writers use cohesive devices that act as threads, binding words, phrases, clauses, sentences and paragraphs to make a text coherent. These devices operate as signposts for the reader, signalling how different parts of a text relate to each other. If phrases and clauses are the building blocks of sentences, then cohesion is what pulls all these different elements together to form a whole, coherent text.

Typical cohesive devices (and we've met most of these already) include the following:

Cohesive devices	How they support cohesion
Conjunctions	Conjunctions link words, phrases and clauses, typically within a sentence. • We tried to attach the wires, <u>but</u> the circuit was broken. • <u>Although</u> we had attached the wires, the bulb did not light up.
Conjunctive adverbials	Conjunctive adverbials link ideas and information within and across sentences and paragraphs. Particular adverbials typically support cohesion in different types of writing: adverbials of contrast (*on the other hand, however, alternatively*) can support a balanced argument, while adverbials of time (*firstly, next, finally*) are often used in instructions or recounts where chronology is the main organising principle. • If the road is not built, there will be more traffic congestion. <u>Consequently</u>, air pollution will increase and. . . • <u>In conclusion</u>, I believe that. . .
Pronouns	Pronouns refer backwards to a noun or noun phrase already mentioned as well as forwards to a noun or noun phrase not yet mentioned. They help to avoid unnecessary repetition. • <u>The stray dog</u> whimpered pitifully. <u>It</u> was hungry. • As <u>she</u> gazed out of the window, <u>Sal</u> wondered when Jimmy would return. Demonstrative pronouns (*this, that, these, those*) are particularly helpful in supporting cohesion: • Although we had attached the wires, the bulb did not light up. <u>This</u> was because. . . • <u>These</u> are all good reasons why. . .
Ellipsis	Ellipsis avoids unnecessary repetition by omitting words that have already been used. It is common in conversation, but is also used in writing. The reader has to 'fill in the gaps'. • I love swimming – I always have (loved swimming). • Sarah bought some cheese and (Sarah bought some) apples.
Determiners	Determiners specify a noun or noun phrase. Demonstrative determiners (*this, that, these, those*) are particularly helpful in supporting cohesion: • <u>These</u> experiments all prove that. . . • <u>My second</u> argument is that. . .
Repetition and synonyms	Repetition can be effective when used deliberately. Alternatively, synonyms can be used to create thematic linkage without repeating the same word. • Following last month's spate of <u>crime</u> which included the <u>theft</u> of a lawnmower and two bicycles from **garden sheds**, residents are being urged to secure their **outbuildings**.
Tense consistency	We'll look at this on the next double-page spread.

Teaching about cohesion

There's very little new grammatical content that you need to teach for cohesion, so you'll need to focus more on teaching pupils how to deploy the grammar they've already been taught to make their writing cohesive.

The most obvious way to do this is by sharing examples of different texts and exploring the features that make them cohesive. It's important that pupils are able to explore complete texts and longer pieces of writing rather than short extracts, since they need to see how cohesion works across several paragraphs or a whole text. Simple devices, such as linking the ending back to the opening, and making sure that paragraphs – especially in non-narrative writing – have clear topic sentences, contribute to cohesion.

You could take a page from a novel or non-fiction text and display it on a visualiser or whiteboard. Annotate the cohesive devices, perhaps using a different colour to signal each type of device (pronouns, adverbials etc.).

Alternatively, remove some of the cohesive devices and ask pupils to help you edit the text to improve cohesion, perhaps by using a simple checklist of cohesive 'tools' based on the grid on the opposite page. Once edited, compare your version to the original. (You could use a similar approach in a guided reading session by annotating a shared text or by asking pupils to identify cohesive devices and discussing the way they signpost the reader.)

Modelled and shared writing are key approaches for teaching pupils how to make their writing cohesive. By modelling writing, you can actively demonstrate how to read back over what you've written, while looking ahead to what will come next. As you do this, you can think aloud as you consider whether your writing is sufficiently cohesive. If pupils tend to produce writing that lacks cohesion, work with them in small focused guided groups to edit a piece of writing to make it more cohesive.

One aspect of cohesion that does merit explicit teaching relates to pronouns. Pronouns typically refer back to a noun or noun phrase (this is known as anaphoric reference), but they can also refer forwards (this is known as cataphoric reference). Cataphoric reference is a particularly useful technique to teach your pupils when they want to create an element of intrigue in their narrative writing. It's not necessary for your pupils to know the terminology, but the technique is well worth teaching. You can model this or draw attention to it in a shared text.

> As <u>he</u> rounded the corner at speed, <u>he</u> almost collided with Mr Greaves, the school caretaker, who was just about to lock the school gates. <u>Sam</u> was in a hurry to get home.

Notice how the noun (Sam) is withheld to create interest and an element of suspense.

WHEN MIGHT WE NEED TO USE COHESION IN WRITING?

All writing needs to be cohesive if readers are to follow its thread and understand its intention. Cohesion is perhaps even more important in non-fiction writing (such as argument, persuasion, information and explanation), where there may not be a narrative thread or an obvious chronological sequence to follow.

What you need to know about tense

We've already looked at verbs and verb forms in the first chapter. Here we'll look at the way they can be used to indicate the time frame of an event or action: this is what we mean when we talk about tense.

There are two tenses in English: the past and the present.

Present tense	The simple present is formed from the base form of the verb. You'll remember that the –s form is used to form the simple present in the third-person singular.
	<div align="center">I dream/he dreams</div>
	The present progressive (also referred to as the present continuous) is formed from the present tense of the auxiliary verb 'be' plus the –ing form of the main (lexical) verb. It typically indicates an action in progress.
	<div align="center">I am dreaming/she is dreaming/we are dreaming</div>
Past tense	The simple past (sometimes referred to as the preterite) is formed from the –ed form of the verb (but remember that irregular verbs take other forms).
	<div align="center">We looked/they sang</div>
	The past progressive (also referred to as the past continuous) is formed from the past tense of the auxiliary verb 'be' plus the –ing form of the main (lexical) verb. It typically indicates an action in progress in the past.
	<div align="center">She was singing/they were singing</div>
	The present perfect is formed from 'have' plus the –ed form (past participle) of the main verb. It is unusual in that it indicates an action that started in the past but continues in (or is still relevant to) the present time.
	<div align="center">I have walked for miles.</div>
	The past perfect is formed from 'had' plus the –ed form (past participle) of the main verb. It indicates an action that started in the past and continued to another point in the past.
	<div align="center">They had walked for miles before they saw the sign.</div>
	It is also possible to combine the progressive and perfect forms:
	<div align="center">It has been snowing. It had been raining all week.</div>

Many grammarians refer to the simple, progressive and perfect forms as 'aspects' since they indicate the writer's perspective of the time frame of the actions or events being described.

Unlike some other languages, there is no specific future tense in English, so we have to find other ways to express future time, such as using a modal verb (*Sarah will join the cadets next year; I'll go home soon*). Other ways include using the simple present (*We travel tomorrow*), the present progressive (*I am staying with friends in Madrid next year*) or 'be going to' (*We are going to watch a film tonight*).

Teaching about tense

The main issue you'll need to address is tense consistency. Sometimes, pupils switch inappropriately from the past to the present tense (or vice versa) in their writing, especially if they get carried away with a strong narrative thread in a story, or don't have a firm grasp of a particular text type. If your pupils tend to do this, it's worth exploring it explicitly as a class activity. You might display a piece of writing on a visualiser and model how to edit for tense consistency. Alternatively, if only a few pupils need support, you could work with them in a small guided group.

It's likely that specific attention to editing will resolve the issue over time. Editing is a key writing skill that needs to be taught: you'll want to reinforce it regularly alongside clear expectations that pupils will edit and proofread their own work as part of the writing process.

Of course, tense consistency doesn't mean that writing needs to use the same tense throughout. Consider the appropriate shifts in tense in the following passage:

> The team's star player <u>scored</u> two goals at yesterday's match. A keen footballer since childhood, she <u>has been training</u> hard and <u>is</u> now one of our best young centre-forwards.

You might discuss the way writers use tense to create time shifts in novels – to signal flashbacks or to replay memories. Alternatively, a letter of complaint might use the present tense to express dissatisfaction, but shift to the past tense to recount the incident that provoked the complaint.

Tense can be more complex than it seems, and the relationship between the verb form and the time frame it indicates is not always straightforward. For example, the simple present can be used in other ways:

- To represent facts that are timeless:
  Madrid is the capital of Spain.
  Chalk is a type of rock.

- To create a sense of immediacy in oral narratives (referred to as the historic present):
  So she comes into the shop this morning, and she asks me if I've got any tinned fish, and I turn around to look on the shelf, and just as I'm about to. . .

- In newspaper headlines to report events that have already taken place:
  England manager resigns!
  Teenager rescues dog from river!

You might invest some class time in exploring the effect of using different verb forms, such as the progressive and the perfect forms, in contrast with the simple present and past forms. You might give pupils a selection of sentences that have the same basic content, but use different verb forms, and ask them to discuss the differences in meaning. You could explore this through drama or role play, by asking pupils to improvise a short scene depicting the events leading up to each sentence.

- The old lady <u>looked</u> out of her window when she heard the noise.
- The old lady <u>was looking</u> out of her window when she heard the noise.
- The old lady <u>had been looking</u> out of her window when she heard the noise.

WHEN MIGHT WE NEED TO USE TENSE IN WRITING?

Whenever we use verbs, we need to think about tense. Appropriate choice of tense is important in all writing, and shifts in tense need to be handled particularly effectively to make our meaning clear.

What you need to know about levels of formality

As writers, we have to make choices which are largely determined by three key considerations:

- Purpose – why am I writing this?
- Audience – who am I writing this for?
- Form (or text type) – what kind of writing is appropriate in this context?

This chapter deals with the way we draw on vocabulary and grammatical structures to adapt our writing for different purposes and audiences, particularly when writing in more formal contexts.

There is a section on writing in an informal style as well as a section on writing in a formal style. We should note, however, that language is rarely simply formal or informal: it tends to sit on a continuum, which is why it's helpful to think about different levels of formality.

Standard English is covered separately: while it's typically associated with more formal speech and writing, it's important that children not only know how to use it, but when to use it, and – of course – when a non-Standard form might be more appropriate.

The passive voice and the subjunctive are also included in this chapter. Although formality is not their prime function, they can be drawn on to create a more formal style in writing, particularly in the way they enable us to present information in different ways to the reader.

The main thing is for young writers to have choices: the choice to use Standard English or a regional dialect; the choice to use an informal, conversational style or a more formal style; the choice to present information in the passive voice or the active voice; the choice to use the subjunctive or not. Above all, they need to understand how to exercise these choices in the context of their writing, dependent on their purpose and intended audience. For example, if children are only ever exposed to informal language, they will be limited as writers, unable to adapt and respond flexibly to different contexts, audiences and purposes.

Register also deserves a mention here. This is the term we tend to use when referring to the specific language (typically vocabulary) used by particular groups or professions when talking or writing about their own field of interest and expertise. Legalese, for example, is the specialised language used by lawyers that most of us without a legal background may struggle to comprehend. You'll be able to think of others: teachers, for example, use particular words and expressions when talking about pedagogy and the curriculum which others may not be familiar with.

For many children, school is the place where they are likely to be exposed to the range of opportunities – through reading and writing and talk – that equip them to become flexible language users.

Teaching about levels of formality

You can draw on pupils' implicit understanding of different types of writing by sharing a number of fragments (such as those in the grid below) and asking them what they can deduce about the intended audience, purpose and context. Then ask them how they know. You might ask them to choose one such fragment and continue it in the same style, adopting the same level of formality and register.

Alternatively, you could take a traditional tale and ask them to rewrite it in a different style. For example, ask them to rewrite *Little Red Riding Hood* from the point of view of the wolf. Another idea might be to ask them to use a different form (or text type), for example by writing a newspaper headline reporting the attacks on the three little pigs, or a crime scene report for the 'break-in' at the house of the three bears.

We are pleased to enclose a cheque for £25.99 as reimbursement for your faulty goods. Please accept our apologies for the inconvenience caused by the. . .	I would never have dreamed that I would one day be a famous musician. My family wasn't particularly well-off, and my mother held down several jobs just to make ends meet. . .
Sara has continued to work hard this term. She has made good progress with her throwing and catching skills, and has participated in a number of competitive sports, such as. . .	To discover whether metal conducts electricity, first we. . .
A forty-two-year-old woman was in police custody last night after an incident outside a supermarket in which three trolleys were damaged. . .	It all started when I woke up last Thursday morning, looked in the mirror, and realised that I'd turned into a frog. . .
In Victorian times, people were either very rich or very poor. It was not unusual for children to be sent to work in. . .	If you could just donate £5 a month to this worthy cause, you would be helping. . .
This latest novel from the best-selling children's writer is one of her best. The action-packed storyline keeps you in suspense from the very start. . .	Freddie tip-toed up the stairs and turned on the landing light. He listened for the sound of his father's snoring. Nothing. . .

What you need to know about the active and the passive voice

We have a choice of two 'voices' – active or passive – and this choice affects the way we present information in a clause. The active voice is far more frequently used in both speech and writing, whereas the passive voice is much less frequently used.

Active voice	Passive voice
The subject and the 'doer' (agent) are one and the same.	The subject is the recipient of the action, or the thing that is affected by the action.
<u>Billy</u> broke Mum's china vase. <u>The headteacher</u> is observing my lesson next week.	<center><u>Mum's china vase</u> was broken by Billy.</center> <center><u>My lesson</u> is being observed by the headteacher next week.</center> The preposition phrase (usually headed up by the preposition 'by') indicates the 'doer' – or agent. Its use is optional. <center>Mum's china vase was broken.</center> <center>My lesson is being observed next week.</center>

Changing from active to passive:

1. The subject in the active clause (Billy/the headteacher) moves to the end in the passive clause. Although it continues to be the agent, it is no longer the subject of the clause. It is introduced by the preposition 'by'.

    <u>Billy</u> broke Mum's china vase.
    Mum's china vase was broken by <u>Billy</u>.
    <u>The headteacher</u> is observing my lesson next week.
    My lesson is being observed by <u>the headteacher</u> next week.

2. The object of the active clause (Mum's china vase/my lesson) moves to the front in the passive clause, where it becomes the subject.

    Billy broke <u>Mum's china vase</u>.
    <u>Mum's china vase</u> was broken by Billy.
    The headteacher is observing <u>my lesson</u> next week.
    <u>My lesson</u> is being observed by the headteacher next week.

3. The verb 'to be' is put into the same tense as the verb in the active clause (broke/is observing). The past (–ed) participle of the verb in the active clause is added.

    Mum's china vase <u>was broken</u> by Billy.
    My lesson <u>is being observed</u> by the headteacher next week.

It's possible to form the passive using 'get' and 'have', and these are often referred to as 'pseudo' passives. The 'get' passive is not generally considered appropriate in formal writing.

I <u>got expelled</u> from school for bad behaviour.
I <u>had</u> my hair <u>coloured</u> by the salon's top stylist.

(Take care not to confuse a 'have' passive with the perfect form, which also uses 'have/had'.)

Teaching about the active and the passive voice

You could use an investigative approach and ask pupils to discuss the difference in the way information is presented in active and passive sentences. It might be best to focus on a specific reason for using the passive, such as building suspense, or sounding authoritative. These sentences all use the passive to avoid owning up to something awkward or embarrassing:

Active	Passive
The year 4 team beat us in the final.	We were beaten in the final.
Dad spilt some red paint on the carpet.	Some red paint was spilt on the carpet.
Jamie has eaten the entire chocolate cake.	The entire chocolate cake has been eaten.
I've just smashed your window.	Your window has just been smashed.

You could look at the way passives are used in a formal report. Try rewriting it using the active voice and discuss the effect. Once you've taught pupils about the passive, it's really important to give them the opportunity and the need to use it, so you'll need to think about writing tasks where the passive would be appropriate.

WHEN MIGHT WE NEED TO USE THE ACTIVE AND THE PASSIVE VOICE IN WRITING?

The active voice is more immediate and places the focus on the 'doer' (agent). It's the voice that's most commonly used, so it's more important to think about when we might make a conscious decision to use the passive voice. The passive tends to place less focus on the agent and more on the actual action or event. Writers often choose an agentless passive for the following reasons:

1. To build suspense in narrative writing by hiding the agent:

- The window <u>had been left</u> slightly ajar. Millicent was certain that she had closed it last night. . .
- The major checked his cabinet but – as he feared – his old army pistol <u>had been removed</u>. . .

2. When the agent is either unknown or unimportant:

- The warehouse <u>was burgled</u> last night.
- The liquid <u>was poured</u> into the test tube.

3. To sound authoritative and convincing:

- Cycling <u>is not permitted</u> in the shopping centre.
- Fitness can <u>be improved</u> in just three weeks!

4. When we want to avoid responsibility or blame for an action:

- The school fair <u>was cancelled</u> at very short notice.
- The decision <u>has been taken</u> to cancel the concert.

5. For succinctness, typically in newspaper headlines (the verb 'be' is implied):

- Pensioner robbed!
- Man arrested for murder.

6. To create a more impersonal style:

- It <u>is believed</u> that many more families will holiday at home this year.
- Tickets can <u>be collected</u> from the school office.

What you need to know about the subjunctive

The subjunctive is rarely used in English. It is mostly associated with very formal – and sometimes archaic – styles. It is typically used in academic, legal or literary texts. Some subjunctive forms are formulaic, such as *God save the Queen*. Interestingly, the subjunctive tends to be quite widely used in America.

To understand the subjunctive, we need to know that a verb form can indicate one of three 'moods':

1. The <u>indicative</u> mood expresses factual meaning.

> The horses galloped across the field.
> The snow fell heavily during the night.

2. The <u>imperative</u> mood expresses directive meaning (such as commands).

> Sit down, please.
> Shuffle the cards and lay them face down.

3. The <u>subjunctive</u> mood expresses unfulfilled or desired states, events or actions (typically with some conditional subordinators such as *if, unless, on condition that*).

> The subjunctive can also express compulsion or necessity (typically after verbs such as *suggest, recommend, request, require, propose, demand, insist, stipulate* and expressions such as *it is important/essential that. . .*). When it is used in this way, it is often referred to as the mandative subjunctive.

The subjunctive has a present tense and a past tense form:

*   In the present tense, it uses the base form of the verb. In other words, the third-person singular (he, she, it) does not take the usual –s ending, and this also applies to irregular verbs. The verb 'to be' is always 'be' (rather than *am, are, is*). The negative form takes 'not' plus the base form of the verb.

> The governors insisted that the headteacher <u>take</u> a long holiday.
> We recommend that she <u>go</u> as soon as possible.
> It is essential that they <u>be</u> completely satisfied with the arrangements.
> She insisted that he <u>not disturb</u> her.

*   In the past tense, the verb 'to be' takes the form 'were' (rather than 'was').

> I wouldn't do that, if I <u>were</u> you.
> I wish she <u>were</u> here now!
> If I <u>were</u> you, I'd go and apologise.
> The toddler looked as though it <u>were</u> about to burst into tears.

Teaching about the subjunctive

You could use an investigative approach, and ask pupils to discuss the differences between a number of sentences that use either the indicative or the subjunctive. Remember that you'll need enough examples for the pattern to be apparent so that pupils can generalise from the examples given. Once they have identified the difference, you'll need to provide a simple explanation of the subjunctive.

They insist that she resign today.	They insist that she resigns today.
We suggest that he leave tomorrow.	We suggest that he leaves tomorrow.
I demand that she stay here.	I demand that she stays here.
We propose that he start at once.	We propose that he starts at once.
I recommend that it stop now.	I recommend that it stops now.

You could display a sentence that uses the subjunctive on the visualiser or whiteboard and model how to express the same meaning using a modal verb instead of the subjunctive:

> *The governors insist that the headteacher <u>take</u> a holiday in August.*
> *The governors insist that the headteacher <u>should take</u> a holiday in August.*

You could point out the way the subjunctive is used in books you're reading with the class, although you may have to look carefully for texts that make use of it.

WHEN MIGHT WE NEED TO USE THE SUBJUNCTIVE IN WRITING?

We can be fluent and confident writers without ever using the subjunctive. However, it can create a more formal style in some writing, and it's certainly helpful if children can recognise and understand it when they encounter it in their reading.

What you need to know about Standard English

- Standard English is a dialect, even though it's not linked to any particular geographical region.
- It can be spoken with any accent.
- It tends to be associated with more formal speech and writing; however, it would be possible to use Standard English in informal writing, and non-Standard English in relatively formal writing.
- There are many regional dialects (non-Standard English) that differ linguistically from Standard English. Non-Standard forms are not inferior to Standard English.
- Standard English is the dialect used in education and publishing, as well as the one that's taught to non-native learners of English. It is used globally, and carries a very definite element of social and academic prestige.

Actually, there aren't very many differences between Standard English and other non-Standard forms: most relate to verb forms which, interestingly, tend to be more regularised in non-Standard dialects than in Standard English. Some of the main differences can be found in the table below.

Grammatical feature	Standard English	Non-Standard forms
Some non-Standard forms regularise simple present verb forms, opting for the –s form or the base form throughout.	He goes there every day. They go there every week.	He go there every day. They goes there every week.
Some non-Standard forms regularise the simple past form of the verb 'be'.	I was expecting you hours ago. We were best friends.	I were expecting you hours ago. We was best friends.
Some non-Standard forms use the –ed (past participle) form of the verb for the simple past, typically with irregular verbs.	I saw you in town today. We did our homework on time.	I seen you in town today. We done our homework on time.
Some non-Standard forms use the base form of the verb for the simple past, typically with irregular verbs.	He gave it to me. He told her to keep it. I saw him last week in the park.	He give it to me. He tell her to keep it. I see him last week in the park.
Some non-Standard forms use multiple negation (or double negatives).	I haven't got any. We didn't do anything. (We did nothing.) She didn't see anybody. (She saw nobody.)	I ain't got none. We didn't do nothing. She didn't see nobody.
Some non-Standard forms use 'ain't' to form the negative of the verbs 'be' and 'have' in the simple present.	That isn't fair. I am not going. She hasn't got any.	That ain't fair. I ain't going. She ain't got none.
There are some differences between Standard English and non-Standard forms in the way they use demonstrative determiners, relative pronouns and reflexive pronouns.	Those cars are flashy! The shoes that I like are in the sale. He forced himself to go. They went by themselves.	Them cars are flashy! The shoes what I like are in the sale. He forced hisself to go. They went by theirselves.

Teaching about Standard English

Teaching about Standard English is about giving children choice, so that they can use Standard English when they need to. Most children are likely to use some form of non-Standard English at home, so it's vital to be sensitive to this and respectful of it.

You might incorporate some research on the origins of Standard English into topic work or as part of a history study. Until the fourteenth century, there were huge variations in regional dialect, with differences in grammar and vocabulary which meant that people living in one part of the country would have had considerable difficulty in understanding people from a different region.

A gradual move towards standardisation was already underway during the fourteenth and fifteenth centuries, and this was accelerated when William Caxton set up his printing press in the late fifteenth century. Caxton was a businessman and a Londoner, so when he had to decide which dialect to use in print, it must have seemed logical to opt for the East Midlands dialect which encompassed the two great seats of learning in Oxford and Cambridge as well as the political and commercial hub in London. Printing helped to spread the dialect further and make it more permanent, enabling it to become the standard written form of English today.

Although not required by the national curriculum, it would be really worthwhile to devote some teaching time to non-Standard dialects, not least because it's easier to teach children about Standard English if they can relate it to non-Standard forms. If you teach in an area where children use a distinctive regional dialect, this could be a really rich source of language study, drawing on local culture and oral history.

Probably the best way to teach about Standard English is to explore a range of texts that use both Standard English and regional dialects. Many novels recreate regional dialects in dialogue, but play scripts and poetry also provide rich material.

You might consider a range of text types for different audiences and purposes, and ask pupils to consider whether Standard English would be appropriate or not.

A letter of complaint to a store manager about a faulty toy
A personal diary
A travel journal in the form of a blog
A play script
A story that incorporates authentic regional dialogue
An email to a friend
A conversation in the playground with a group of friends
A party invitation
A report for a local newspaper
A radio football commentary
A television interview with a well-known local celebrity

WHEN MIGHT WE NEED TO USE STANDARD ENGLISH IN WRITING?

It is generally considered appropriate to use Standard English in more formal written contexts. Unless a writer makes a definite choice to use a regional dialect (for example, to create a vivid sense of character or location), relatively formal writing for an unknown reader typically requires Standard English. The most important thing is for children to have the choice: to know how and when to use Standard English.

What you need to know about writing in an informal style

When we write in an informal style, we tend to use some of the characteristics of spoken language to adopt a friendly, conversational manner.

However, written language is not the same as spoken language, as any transcript of talk will demonstrate. Talk is ephemeral and generally more spontaneous than writing; it tends to be more interactive and responsive to our listener or audience. In contrast, writing is more permanent and can be planned and edited. As writers, we have to engage with unknown and potentially remote readers. When we adopt an informal style in writing, we can use the type of vocabulary and grammatical structures that seem to echo speech to establish a more intimate relationship with our reader.

Some of the features that are typically used to adopt an informal style include the following:

Feature	Examples
Contracted forms in verb phrases	<u>I'm</u> off now. If only you <u>could've</u> stayed a bit longer. <u>It'd</u> be great if Tom could come too. <u>We'll</u> head off in a moment. <u>Here's</u> your cup of tea. <u>What's</u> up?
Abbreviations or contracted forms of words	I can't come '<u>cos</u> I've got homework tonight. Shall we take a <u>photo</u> of the sunset? <u>Phone</u> me! Tom rides his <u>bike</u> to school. <u>Thanks</u> for that!
Question tags	This is lovely, <u>isn't it</u>? You will come, <u>won't you</u>?
Multi-word verbs (including phrasal and prepositional verbs)	Find out (rather than 'discover') Ask for (rather than 'request') Give in (rather than 'concede')
Ellipsis	So much to tell you. Have to go now!
'Got' passives	The warehouse <u>got burgled</u> last night. Our team <u>gets beaten</u> every time it plays away.
First person	I/we
Direct address to the reader	<u>You</u> know the feeling. . . Wouldn't <u>you</u> like to know. . .
Vague language	That's such a <u>nice sort of thing</u> to say. I've got so much <u>stuff</u> in here.
Vernacular language, including slang and idioms	The <u>kids</u> were <u>always getting into scrapes</u> at home. <u>That's really cool</u>! I'm such a computer <u>geek</u>! Mick's <u>over the moon</u> with his new bike. He really didn't <u>have a leg to stand on</u>.
Discourse markers commonly used in spoken language	Well. . . Right. . . You see. . . Anyway. . . Okay. . .

Teaching about writing in an informal style

For the most part, children tend to know intuitively how to use an informal style: it's their default model, used in most social interactions with friends and family at home and – to a large extent – at school. However, it's still important to unpick some of the features that help us to write in an informal style so that we can do so consciously when we need to.

Of course, language isn't simply either formal or informal – it sits on a continuum. This is why it's helpful to think about different levels of formality. You could explore this with pupils by giving them a set of words or phrases that have the same basic meaning, and ask them to rank them according to their degree of formality. They could do this on a scale of 1–10 (with one being 'very informal' and 10 being 'very formal'), or they could simply put them in order of formality. This is best done in pairs or small groups to facilitate discussion about the decisions they make.

Hello	Hiya	Morning	Dear Ms Smith	To whom it may concern
Dear Sally	Good morning	Dear Madam	Dear Sir or Madam	Hi

Please may I have a coffee?	I'd like a coffee, please.
Coffee – white – no sugar.	Can I get a coffee? Thanks.
A cup of coffee, if you please.	Could I have a coffee, please?

Hi Sue, Had a really great time yesterday. Would love to meet up again and perhaps go for a pizza. Do you fancy that? Speak soon! Bob	Dear Susan, Thank you so much for lunch yesterday; it was most enjoyable. I'd very much like to see you again and wondered whether you might like to join me for dinner one evening? I'll await your reply. Robert

WHEN MIGHT WE NEED TO USE AN INFORMAL STYLE IN WRITING?

An informal style may well be appropriate in a first-person recount, such as a diary, autobiography or blog, or a personal email or letter. Any attempt to recreate realistic dialogue, for example in a story or play script, is likely to require an informal style. What's important is that children are able to adopt an informal style intentionally rather than having no other option available to them.

What you need to know about writing in a formal style

Standard English is likely to be appropriate in most formal writing. Other features that are typically used to adopt a formal style include the following:

Feature	Examples
Appropriate choice of modals in certain contexts	We <u>shall</u> try our best. <u>May</u> I have another piece of cake? <u>Might</u> I ask why this is not allowed? I <u>should</u> like to offer my sincere condolences.
Lexical verbs rather than multi-word verbs	Discover (rather than 'find out') Request (rather than 'ask for') Concede (rather than 'give up')
Agentless passives, especially with the dummy subject 'it'	It <u>is believed</u> that more families will holiday at home this year. It <u>is considered</u> impolite to talk whilst eating.
Nominalisation	The <u>departure</u> of the guests caused much <u>relief</u>. The <u>success</u> of the school concert is a <u>cause</u> for <u>celebration</u>.
The personal pronoun 'one'	<u>One</u> might expect better service in this restaurant. <u>One</u> feels more comfortable in <u>one's</u> own home.
The subjunctive	The club's owner demanded that the manager <u>resign</u>. I recommend that she <u>leave</u> at once.
Avoidance of preposition stranding	For whom are you looking? (Who are you looking for?) To which pupils are you referring? (Which pupils are you referring to?)
Inversion of wording (replacing the subordinating conjunction 'if') in some conditional clauses	<u>Had I seen</u> her, I would have said something. (<u>If I'd seen</u> her, I'd have said something.) <u>Should you consider</u> accepting this position, we'd be delighted. (<u>If you'd consider</u> accepting this position, we'd be delighted.)
Avoidance of colloquial vocabulary, contractions and abbreviations	The <u>children</u> were <u>constantly misbehaving</u> at home. <u>That is most interesting</u>. I <u>do not</u> wish to discuss this any further. <u>We will</u> talk about this later. The <u>telephone</u> rang in the middle of the night.

Teaching about writing in a formal style

Children are likely to have more limited exposure to formal writing and fewer opportunities to use it, so the encounters and experiences you provide at school are hugely important. It's easy to assume that children can simply recognise when some writing sounds more formal than other writing – while this may be true, it's important to teach some of the vocabulary and grammatical features that enable us to adopt a more formal style. There is no requirement to teach all of the features in the grid on the opposite page, but judicious selection of those that seem most appropriate for your pupils will give them the tools they need to adopt a suitably formal style that's appropriate to a formal context, audience and purpose.

You might share a piece of relatively formal writing, such as a letter of application, and include one or two informal features. Ask pupils to identify those that seem inappropriate for a formal context. Most importantly, ask them to explain why, and then ask them to suggest more appropriate wording.

Less formal	More formal
I'm really keen to be your new pastry chef. I'm pretty good at making cakes and everyone raves about my Victoria sponge. . .	I am writing to express my interest in the post of pastry chef at Buckingham Palace. I am able to offer a wealth of experience. . .

Alternatively, you could give pupils a handful of short texts written for different audiences, ranging from the very informal to the very formal. Ask them to rank them according to their level of formality, and identify the features that mark them out as being particularly formal.

When it comes to teaching pupils how to write in a formal style, modelling is likely to be one of the best approaches. The sequence for teaching writing can be used as follows:

- Share good models and explore their features and conventions.
- Actively demonstrate the writing process, thinking aloud as you compose.
- Invite pupils to share in the composition, sifting and evaluating their responses.
- Support first attempts, for example, through guided group work or scaffolding.
- Provide choices for independent application.

Give pupils opportunities to use more formal spoken language, for example formal debate or a presentation to another class. You could use role play, for example, by staging a scenario such as complaining about a faulty item or putting a character from a novel on trial. Formal talk can be modelled too, with oral sentence starters to support pupils as they try out less familiar language.

WHEN MIGHT WE NEED TO USE A FORMAL STYLE IN WRITING?

This depends entirely on context, audience and purpose. Letters of application or complaint are likely to require a formal style, as are some non-fiction texts such as reports, formal argument or evaluation where our relationship with the reader needs to be objective, polite or authoritative.

What you need to know about punctuation

Grammar and punctuation are so closely integrated that it would seem strange not to include a chapter on punctuation in this book. This chapter deals with the main forms of punctuation that you'll need to teach in the primary classroom.

Most dictionary definitions of punctuation make reference to the marks that separate sentences and their elements (graphemes, words, phrases and clauses), and to their function in clarifying meaning. The emphasis, therefore, is firmly on the grammatical and semantic functions of punctuation.

Of course, this wasn't always the case. In Ancient Greece and Rome, when oratory and rhetoric were highly prized skills, speakers used to annotate their speeches to show where they should pause and when they should breathe, rather like musical notation. You may have been taught yourself at some point that commas show you where to breathe, although this is not particularly helpful advice today.

Centuries later, early manuscripts began to use spacing and dots between words to aid legibility. Gradually, other punctuation marks were introduced, until conventions became fixed by the advent of printing in the fifteenth century (although new marks continued to appear, for example, the colon and the semi-colon in the sixteenth century). With an increasingly literate population, the purpose of punctuation shifted from supporting oratory to supporting meaning by focusing on separating (or joining) grammatical elements of the sentence.

You could say that we've come back to where we started, with website addresses now omitting spacing between words and some text messaging omitting punctuation altogether. Some punctuation marks are less widely used today than in the past, while new ones are appearing, such as the inventive and personalised use of emoji and emoticons.

Punctuation is perhaps best seen as a set of conventions. Although there are rules, there is still disagreement about some of them, such as the use of the serial comma. And much punctuation usage does come down to personal and stylistic choice – for example, whether we favour a 'heavy' or 'light' approach to punctuation. Numerous style guides have their say too.

Some punctuation continues to confuse writers well into adulthood (think of the 'greengrocer's apostrophe'): such visible errors can invite scorn and lead to talk about falling standards. Others take a more liberal approach to punctuation: text messaging often leaves out punctuation completely, as does some critically renowned poetry. However, if we're going to break the rules or adapt the conventions for literary and creative effect, or simply for economy, we need to know what they are in the first place.

Teaching about punctuation

Punctuation, along with spelling and capitalisation, comes under the definition of orthography rather than grammar, as it has more to do with the way we write things down than the structure of the language itself.

When we talk, we can pause, repeat things and clarify our meaning in response to feedback from our listeners. We can use intonation to convey nuances of meaning. We don't necessarily speak in sentences, but more typically fragments composed of single words, phrases and clauses.

However, when we write, we use the convention of punctuation to guide our (usually unknown and remote) reader, to help them navigate our writing and understand what we mean to say. Commas and hyphens, for example, both play an important role in clarifying meaning and avoiding ambiguity. Think about the difference the hyphen makes in 'man-eating shark', and the impact of the commas on the meaning of these two sentences:

> The passengers who went down with a severe sickness bug are suing the tour operator.
>
> The passengers, who went down with a severe sickness bug, are suing the tour operator.

It's helpful for children to know when punctuation is just right or wrong (for example, the punctuation of speech) and when they have a choice. For example, punctuation choices can convey formality (semi-colons and colons can look impressive in letters of application) or informality (dashes convey a more unplanned, speechlike impression).

Punctuation 'fans' can be used to surface some of those choices and the meanings they convey. (These are available commercially, but schools can also make their own.) They can be particularly effective during shared writing when you pause to deliberate on a punctuation choice and ask pupils to hold up their fans to show the punctuation they would use.

When you're teaching children about punctuation, it's worth considering the following points:

1. Punctuation, like grammar, is best taught in the context of writing, rather than through decontextualised exercises. This way, we can keep the focus on the way it supports the reader's understanding.

2. Reading and talk both support the teaching of punctuation: seeing it in print, and experiencing firsthand the way it helps us as a reader, can prompt us to consider our reader when we write; similarly, thinking about how to write down the ideas in our head, and rehearsing them orally before we write, can help us to shape the meaning we want to convey in writing.

3. Editing and proofreading have a vital part to play in the writing process. Some writers prefer to punctuate during the drafting process; others prefer to go back and refine the punctuation once a section has been composed. Either way, the writer needs to be the first proofreader of the writing, taking responsibility for checking that their intended meaning is clear.

4. The way we respond to punctuation in children's writing is key. Making corrections without explaining them is unhelpful: it's far better to use a child's errors diagnostically to inform teaching, and to pose questions such as, 'What did you mean here? What punctuation might help me to understand what you mean?'

What you need to know about capital letters

Capital letters (also referred to as upper-case letters) serve a number of purposes.

1. They indicate the start of a sentence. This is not a new convention: the beautifully illuminated medieval manuscripts used a large, ornate capital letter at the beginning of a script. Today, we use capital letters to draw attention to the start of a sentence.

    Rosalind woke with a start. She sat up and looked around her. The room looked unfamiliar.

2. They indicate proper nouns (nouns that name specific people, places, events or things). The days of the week and months of the year fall into this category, as do brand names.

    My best friend is Sally Smith.
    We went to France for our holiday.
    We visited the Tower of London.
    Our athletes won lots of medals in the Olympic Games.
    I went swimming on Saturday.
    My birthday is in July.
    We break up next week for the Christmas holidays.
    Julius Caesar was an important figure in the Roman Empire.

3. They indicate the personal pronoun 'I'.

4. They indicate the names of languages and nationalities. (Note that french windows is not capitalised, as they don't necessarily come from France.)

    Today we have art, history and French.
    We have a French student staying with us this summer.
    Our french windows open out into the garden.

5. They indicate important words in titles of books, plays and films (although some publishers only capitalise the first word in a title).

    We are reading *Treasure Island* in year 6.
    My favourite film is *The Wizard of Oz*.

Teaching about capital letters

Once children are familiar with the alphabet and can form distinct upper-case letters, you'll be able to show them how they should be used through their own reading and in their own writing. You might start by writing some of your pupils' names on the board and showing them how they start with a capital letter. It's best to keep it familiar at this stage – use people and places they know and explain that the capital letter shows us these are special names.

Children need to have some understanding of what a sentence is to use a capital letter at the start of one. You really need to teach this in conjunction with full stops, so that full stops and capital letters are seen as the way we demarcate sentences. Children will find it easier to understand that we follow a full stop with a capital letter, and you can reinforce this by always modelling at least two sentences at a time.

You might give pupils a short passage and ask them to put in the capital letters. You could tell them how many to look for, or specify the number of capital letters needed for different purposes, such as capital letters that show the names of people, the names of places, the important words in a title or the start of a new sentence. You could give them small cards in the shape of arrows and ask pupils to put them in the right places, explaining why they made their decisions.

> my best friends are timothy, ben and clara. we are all in the same class. our teacher is mr brown. last friday we went on a school trip to london. we went on a boat on the river thames and we saw a play called charlie and the chocolate factory.

Take every opportunity to draw attention to the way capital letters are used in the books you're reading as a class, asking children what they notice about where the capital letters are and what job they are doing.

WHEN MIGHT WE NEED TO USE CAPITAL LETTERS IN WRITING?

Capital letters have been in use for a very long time, although their use in informal email and text messaging is diminishing. Although it's possible to read and understand writing without capitals, they do add another layer of information for the reader and – in some cases – can help to avoid ambiguity (for example, 'I'm reading English at the University of Reading'). Many style guides warn against overusing capital letters as too many can be quite irritating on the eye.

What you need to know about sentence demarcation

We demarcate sentences with what we call 'end' punctuation to signal to the reader that we have come to the end of a sentence. The full stop (sometimes referred to as a 'period') is the most usual punctuation mark for this, but we can also use a question mark, an exclamation mark or even ellipsis dots when appropriate.

Jamie kicked the ball into the goal.
Jamie kicked the ball into the goal!
Wow! That's amazing!
Did you hear that noise?
How sad that we didn't manage to say goodbye.
What a brilliant performance that was!
The door creaked slowly open. . .
Well, I'm really not sure. . .

We've already looked at sentences with different forms in Chapter 3, but it's worth recapping some points about the options we have for demarcating sentences:

1. Full stops are typically used to demarcate statements and commands, but an exclamation mark can be used to add emotive force, typically in narrative or more informal writing, or to show that a character is shouting.

2. Question marks are used to demarcate direct questions.

3. Exclamation marks are usually used to demarcate exclamations and interjections, although a full stop may sometimes be used to demarcate a less forceful exclamation.

4. Ellipsis dots can be used to suggest a 'trailing away' which might indicate uncertainty, suspense or a cliff hanger. . .

5. Full stops can be used to demarcate single words, fragments and minor sentences. This is quite common in literary texts, advertising and in more informal writing.

6. In *very* informal writing, more than one question mark or exclamation mark might be used for emphasis. There is even a new (and definitely non-standard) punctuation mark known as the interrobang (or interabang), which combines a question mark with an exclamation mark.

7. A comma should never be used to separate sentences. This is a common error known as the 'comma splice'. We'll look at it in more detail shortly.

Teaching about sentence demarcation

It's more helpful to think about full stops as separating sentences rather than ending them. It's understandable that some children don't see the need to demarcate a single 'stand-alone' sentence, since it already looks complete. However, once we begin to write more than one sentence, the need for full stops to mark the boundaries between sentences becomes more apparent. As soon as practicably possible, ask pupils to write two or more consecutive sentences so that there is a clear need to separate them with a full stop.

You could share a short, unpunctuated passage of at least three sentences with the class and ask them to agree where the full stops should go. You could ask them to try reading the passage aloud to each other first, to see how the absence of sentence demarcation makes it difficult to read and obscures the meaning. You could give them three full stops on cards and ask them to put them in the right places, explaining why they made their decisions and what else they would need to change in the passage (capitalisation).

> Tim went to the park with his friends they played on the swings and had a picnic on the grass Tim's mum had packed sandwiches and fruit for everybody

Another effective way to draw attention to the use of punctuation is to ask pupils to use a coloured pen or pencil. This does slow down the writing process, but, for young writers who often need to construct sentences orally first, it can really help. With pupils who are prone to forgetting or omitting punctuation, colour is a useful tool – if there is no or little colour in a passage of writing, it is immediately clear that there is likely to be a punctuation issue. Older pupils can simply overwrite punctuation with a coloured pen when reading back their writing – this is a quick and effective method of checking for accuracy.

An effective approach with older pupils is to make the link between punctuation and drama. If you're working on a soliloquy from Shakespeare, you can ask pupils to pace the text by walking as they read the lines aloud, stopping and turning every time they reach a full stop, question mark or exclamation mark. As well as drawing attention to the demarcation in the text, this approach can also illuminate the character's thought processes, such as confusion, hesitation or indecision. You'll need to clear some space in the classroom for this, or use the school hall.

Older pupils may well need to be reminded about sentence demarcation, long after it has first been taught. Ask pupils to read their writing back to a partner to make sure that their full stops are in the right places, and remind them to keep a careful eye out for any comma splicing.

WHEN MIGHT WE NEED TO USE SENTENCE DEMARCATION IN WRITING

Just as we use spacing to separate words, so we use full stops to separate sentences. When writing consists of more than one sentence (and this is likely to be the case most of the time), demarcation separates the sentences and enables the reader to navigate the text.

What you need to know about apostrophes

The main functions of the apostrophe are to mark contracted forms and to indicate possession.

A contracted form (or contraction) is a way of compressing two words into one, typically in speech and informal writing, usually in verb phrases. Remember to put the apostrophe where the letter or letters have been missed out – not just where the words have been joined (*have'nt* = an error).

Examples of contracted forms	Equivalent full forms
Haven't	Have not
I'm	I am
Could've	Could have
It'd	It had/it would
We'll	We will/we shall
Here's	Here is/here are
What's	What is/what has
There's	There is/there are

It's not just verb phrases that exist as contracted forms, but they are certainly the most common. Other contractions are widely used, such as *o'clock* (*of the clock*), or have morphed into non-contracted forms, such as *Halloween* (*Hallowe'en* from *All Hallows' Eve*).

The apostrophe for possession (also referred to as the genitive case, or the genitive –'s) continues to cause difficulties for children and adults alike. The rules are clear, if a little illogical:

Rule	Examples
• For a singular noun, add 's.	The baby's cot My boss's office Sam's journey
• For a plural noun not ending in –s, add 's.	The children's books The sheep's fleeces Those people's children
• For a plural noun ending in –s, just add an apostrophe.	The ladies' cloakroom His parents' house The dogs' baskets
• For names ending in –s, just add an apostrophe if the extra 's' is not pronounced. If it is pronounced, you can add just an apostrophe or 's.	Dickens' novels James' football James's sister
• For some indefinite pronouns, add 's (or just add an apostrophe for a plural form).	Nobody's fault Someone's ice cream Everybody's dream Each other's problems Others' lives seem so exciting

Possessive pronouns (mine, yours, his, hers, ours, yours, theirs) and possessive determiners (my, your, his, her, its, our, your, their) don't take an apostrophe. The only exception is the possessive pronoun *one's*.

Teaching about apostrophes

There are some common errors associated with apostrophes:

- putting an apostrophe into a straightforward plural word where there is no possession (I like apple's and banana's = an error)
- putting the apostrophe where the words are joined in a contraction rather than where the letter/s have been omitted (*have'nt = an error*)
- confusing words like its/it's and whose/who's.

These errors all come down to an insecure understanding of how and when to use an apostrophe. In some cases, the uncertainty is deep rooted, and is hampered by seemingly illogical rules: why is there no apostrophe in 'its' when used to show possession? The confusion is further compounded when place names drop the apostrophe or use it inconsistently (we see Kings Cross and King's Cross). It can be a minefield for children, and the difficulties often linger into adulthood.

It's advisable to teach the apostrophe for contracted forms first as this is more straightforward. You can make this highly visual and interactive by using the whiteboard or large cards with different letters. Use a large apostrophe to drop into the space vacated by the missing letters. Once you've ascertained that *it's* with an apostrophe is a contracted form of it is/it has, you can reveal a number of sentences and give pupils 'show me' cards with its/it's.

She thinks it's lovely!	The dog chewed on its bone
The cat grooms its kittens	It's nearly home time

This is also a good way of checking their understanding. Ask children who show you the correct answer to explain their thinking. You could do the same with *they're*, *you're* and *there's*. Display them on the learning wall and draw pupils' attention to them frequently.

If you find that children are randomly putting apostrophes into straightforward plural nouns where there is no possession, you might ban them completely while you unpick the misconception. If most of the class are doing this, then it needs further whole-class teaching. If it's a handful of pupils, you can address it through a guided group.

If pupils are struggling to work out whether to put the apostrophe before or after the 's', ask them who owns what. There are likely to be two nouns together, the first one being the owner. Put the apostrophe straight after the name of the owner. You could model this first, and share your thought process. Does this show ownership? Who owns what? Yes – the house belongs to Lucy. Who owns the house? Lucy – so I'll put the apostrophe straight after 'Lucy' and before the 's'.

- I went to Lucy's house for tea.

You might start with names, then build up to other common singular and plural nouns. Be prepared to reinforce the learning regularly until pupils' understanding is secure.

WHEN MIGHT WE NEED TO USE APOSTROPHES IN WRITING?

Some people believe we should do away with apostrophes altogether, while others are quite offended by incorrect usage. Like other forms of punctuation, they do have a role in clarifying meaning.

What you need to know about commas

Commas are used to separate words, phrases and clauses within a sentence. You may have been taught that commas show the reader where to pause or take a breath; while it is true that commas can sometimes function in this way, this is generally not very helpful advice.

Commas help to make the writer's meaning clear to the reader by separating grammatical elements of a sentence. However, there is some variation in the way we choose to use commas, with some writers favouring 'light' punctuation, using commas only when absolutely necessary, and others favouring 'heavy' punctuation, which tends towards greater use of commas. It can sometimes be a matter of personal and stylistic choice.

Commas can be used in many ways and we'll look at some of these ways over the next four pages. We'll look at commas for parenthesis in a separate section.

1.   Commas for 'listing'

Commas can be used to separate words, phrases or clauses in a list. The comma replaces a coordinating conjunction – typically and/or.

- I ordered ham, egg and chips for my lunch.
- Tom packed a pair of pyjamas, a new tube of toothpaste, several paperback novels and a torch.
- We couldn't decide whether to buy Mum a bunch of flowers, a box of chocolates or some perfume.
- She strolled down the lane, walked up the garden path and tapped on the window.
- No running, ducking or diving in or around the swimming pool.

Some people advocate the use of a serial comma (also known as an Oxford comma) before the final 'and'. There are reasons for and against its use, but the trend in B English is to omit it unless it helps to make the meaning clearer:

- I had cereal, bacon and eggs, and coffee for my breakfast.
- She stumbled down the road, picked her way along the overgrown and uneven path, and tapped on the window.

Commas can also be used to separate lists of adjectives. The comma can be replaced by the coordinating conjunction 'and' because the adjectives modify the same thing.

- We had really awful weather on holiday. It was cold, wet and windy all week.
- She picked her way carefully along the overgrown, uneven path.

Don't use a comma in a list of adjectives which don't modify the same thing.

- The powerful Roman army was very successful in battle.
- There are several huge oak trees in our garden.

Notice that 'powerful' modifies 'Roman army' and 'huge' modifies 'oak trees'. A comma could not be replaced by 'and'.

2. Commas after fronted adverbials

In Chapter 2, we noted that adverbials can be moved to the front of a clause and that, when they are, a comma is typically used:

- <u>Without warning</u>, Sally slammed on her brakes.
- <u>After university</u>, Niall decided to go travelling.

It's not essential to use a comma after a fronted adverbial. If the adverbial is short and the meaning is clear, it may not be necessary (you'll remember that an adverbial can consist of a single adverb):

- <u>Yesterday</u> we went to the leisure centre.
- <u>One day</u> I will learn to snorkel.

A comma can affect the way we want a sentence to be read. Notice the way the comma invites a pause in the second sentence, creating a sense of reflection and slowing the pace.

- Sometimes I wonder why I bother!
- Sometimes, I fall asleep and dream that I am flying.

Conjunctive adverbials (adverbials that connect independent clauses) and disjuncts (adverbs that indicate the writer's viewpoint or stance) are typically followed by a comma when they are positioned at the front of a clause:

- It's raining heavily now; <u>however</u>, sunshine is forecast for later in the day.
- <u>Personally</u>, I don't care whether you buy it or not.

3. Commas to mark coordinated clauses

Unless you're an advocate of heavy punctuation, commas aren't typically used before the coordinating conjunction in a coordinated clause, especially if the clauses share the same subject. However, it's usual to put a comma before 'but' when it introduces a clause.

- We turned the corner and saw the most amazing sight!
- Shall we stay at home or go to the party?
- My friends weren't keen, but I really wanted to go to the party.
- I wanted to improve my Spanish, but didn't know where to start.

There isn't really a definitive rule, but the longer the clause, the more likely it is that a comma will help to orientate the reader:

- We headed up into the hills on a narrow, winding, unmade road, and marvelled at the mountain views.
- I ordered bacon and eggs, and then decided that I'd like some toast too.

The shorter the clause and the greater the cohesion between the clauses, the less likely it is that a comma is needed:

- Tom enjoyed playing football and he'd excelled at it since he was a boy.

4. Commas to mark subordinate clauses

It's usual to put a comma after a fronted subordinate clause, and subordinate clauses that are dropped into the middle of a main clause are typically buffered by a pair of commas.

It's not usually necessary to put a comma after a main clause, unless it supports clarity.

- The headteacher decided to finish the meeting early because it was getting late.
- The headteacher, because it was getting late, decided to finish the meeting early.
- Because it was getting late, the headteacher decided to finish the meeting early.

Notice the difference the comma makes to the meaning in the second sentence below:

a. I didn't go to college because I wanted to become a fashion designer.

(In other words, I went to college for another reason.)

b. I didn't go to college, because I wanted to become a fashion designer.

(In other words, I didn't go to college at all. I couldn't study fashion at college.)

5. Commas to mark relative clauses (see Chapter 2)

A pair of commas is always used around a non-defining (non-restrictive) relative clause. This is similar to the way we use a pair of commas for parenthesis: the relative clause provides additional information that is not essential to the meaning and could therefore be simply lifted out of the sentence without affecting its meaning. Like parenthesis, a pair of brackets or dashes could be used instead.

- My friend, who lives in London, is selling her house.
- My cat, which is a Siamese, is called Snooty.
- My cousin, whose wedding we went to last year, is having a baby.

A single comma is used to mark off a sentential relative clause.

- She decided to train to be a hairdresser, which was a really good idea.
- After we'd visited Australia, we travelled on to New Zealand, which was absolutely brilliant!

The comma splice is one of the most common punctuation errors you're likely to see. This is when a writer uses a comma to separate two sentences (or two independent clauses). It is an error.

John is a very good swimmer, he trains every day.

The comma is not strong enough to separate sentences in this way. There are alternatives, depending on how closely you want to link the two clauses:

1. Use a conjunction.
   John is a very good swimmer because he trains every day.
   John is a very good swimmer yet he trains every day.
2. Use a full stop and start a new sentence.
   John is a very good swimmer. He trains every day.
3. Use a semi-colon or colon (as appropriate).
   John is a very good swimmer; he trains every day.
   John is a very good swimmer: he trains every day.

Teaching about commas

Commas in lists can be taught to younger children by working up a fun list (for example, of things they would like to do, or things/people they would like to be). You could log some of their ideas on the board as a vertical list, and then show pupils how to write them in a sentence, using commas to separate the 'items'. Alternatively, you could make this less abstract by showing children different objects and agreeing three or four favourites.

- Ride in a space rocket
- Paint a sunset
- Swim in the sea
- Eat an ice cream
- Dress up as a pirate

> I'd like to ride in a space rocket, eat an ice cream and paint a sunset.

Give pupils a sentence where the meaning is unclear and ask them to add one, or more than one, comma to clarify the meaning. For example, it's not at all clear how many people are involved in this sentence:

> Last week we played with my best friend Sally our next-door neighbour Tom and our two cousins.

You could set pupils a challenge by asking them to insert punctuation to show that there are either six or four people involved.

Last week we played with my best friend, Sally, our next-door neighbour, Tom and our two cousins.	Six people
Last week we played with my best friend Sally, our next-door neighbour Tom, and our two cousins.	Four people: Sally is my best friend and Tom is my next-door neighbour

You could give pupils the sentence printed on cards and ask them to insert commas in different places to change the meaning.

Last week we played with	my best friend	Sally
our next-door neighbour	Tom	and our two cousins.
,	,	,

The comma investigation in Chapter 2 can be used to show pupils how commas are used to buffer fronted subordinate clauses. Alternatively, you could use a similar approach with fronted adverbials (including single adverbs, phrases and clauses) and ask pupils to consider why commas are sometimes used and sometimes not.

WHEN MIGHT WE NEED TO USE COMMAS IN WRITING?

Although many commas are optional, and their use can depend on heavy or light punctuation choices, we really can't do without them in our writing. Commas can show us which parts of a sentence are superfluous, they can help us to navigate a complex piece of writing, and they can clarify meaning and avoid ambiguity. They're pretty essential, really.

What you need to know about punctuation for parenthesis

When we talk about something being 'in parenthesis', we're referring to a word or group of words inserted into a sentence as a kind of afterthought, rather like an 'aside' in a play when the actor speaks directly to the audience. We usually punctuate parenthetical words with a pair of brackets, dashes or commas. (The term 'parentheses' can also be used to describe a pair of brackets.)

The words included in parenthesis usually provide additional, non-essential information and could be removed without affecting the sense of the sentence.

- The festival is held in Arundel (a small town in West Sussex) and draws large crowds during the Bank Holiday weekend.
- The festival is held in Arundel – a small town in West Sussex – and draws large crowds during the Bank Holiday weekend.
- The festival is held in Arundel, a small town in West Sussex, and draws large crowds during the Bank Holiday weekend.

While we have a choice of using brackets, dashes or commas, they can function slightly differently. Brackets and dashes tend to mark a stronger interruption, whereas commas tend to mark a weaker interruption which can appear to be more integrated into the sentence.

- The Battle of the Somme (one of the most senseless and deadly battles of the First World War) was commemorated on its centenary in July 2016.
- The decision to build the new road – and this is my personal opinion – is an absolute disaster.
- This year's school concert was, as always, a great success.

Dashes tend to be used in more informal writing, as they can create a spontaneous, speechlike impression.

- She came running downstairs and tripped – that stair carpet had needed replacing for ages – and that's how she broke her ankle.

A pair of brackets can enclose a complete sentence that's not part of another sentence. When we do this, the punctuation goes inside the brackets.

- The theatre trip was, as always, a great success. (This year, we took sixty children.)

Brackets and dashes can mark off a complete main clause, but a pair of commas can only mark off a subordinate clause, phrase or word.

- We arrived, fortunately, just in time.
- He completed the day's walk, sweating profusely, and decided to go for a swim.

Although brackets, dashes and commas are used in pairs to indicate parenthesis, it is possible to use a single dash – or a single comma – to indicate a parenthetical afterthought when it falls at the end of a sentence.

- The festival is held in Arundel – a small town in West Sussex.
- The festival is held in Arundel, a small town in West Sussex.

Teaching about punctuation for parenthesis

You'll be able to link punctuation for parenthesis with work on relative clauses. You'll remember that non-defining (non-restrictive) relative clauses provide additional information that is not essential to the meaning and could simply be lifted out of the sentence without affecting its meaning. Typically, a pair of commas is used around a non-defining (non-restrictive) relative clause, but a pair of brackets or dashes could be used instead.

If pupils are familiar with non-defining relative clauses, it's worth exploring the different effect of using either commas, dashes or brackets:

- Ronald, who was a very particular child, always took great care with his appearance.
- Ronald – who was a very particular child – always took great care with his appearance.
- Ronald (who was a very particular child) always took great care with his appearance.
- Mount Etna, which is in Sicily, is the tallest active volcano in the world.
- Mount Etna – which is in Sicily – is the tallest active volcano in the world.
- Mount Etna (which is in Sicily) is the tallest active volcano in the world.

If you've already taught your pupils about relative clauses, the logical next step is to show them how other words, phrases and clauses can be used parenthetically. An investigative approach would work well, as would any opportunity to comment on parenthesis through reading. You could take a short information leaflet and use a sentence-combining approach. Give children sections of the text on cards and ask them to combine them, using appropriate punctuation. Their choice of punctuation should provide an important focus for discussion.

St Ives	several miles out to sea
home to a small colony of Grey Atlantic Seals	including the famous Tate St Ives which opened in 1993
it is the home of many painters and sculptors	a seaside town and fishing port in Cornwall
renowned for its art galleries	lies Seal Island
is inundated with tourists during the summer months	just west of St Ives

St Ives, a seaside town and fishing port in Cornwall, is inundated with tourists during the summer months. Renowned for its art galleries, including the famous Tate St Ives which opened in 1993, it is the home of many painters and sculptors. Just west of St Ives, several miles out to sea, lies Seal Island, home to a small colony of Grey Atlantic Seals.

WHEN MIGHT WE NEED TO USE PUNCTUATION FOR PARENTHESIS IN WRITING?

Parenthesis enables us to drop more information into a sentence. Appropriate punctuation shows the reader that it's additional information that could be removed without affecting the basic meaning.

What you need to know about semi-colons

A semi-colon is used to join two independent clauses (or sentences). It's stronger than a comma (which can't join independent clauses) yet not as abrupt as a full stop. It joins two clauses of equal status where there's a sense of balance and coordination. We tend to use a semi-colon to join two clauses that are closely related in meaning. The semi-colon establishes a semantic link – which the reader has to work out – between the two clauses.

- The door hung lopsidedly on one hinge; the plaster was crumbling and damp.

It would, of course, be possible to simply write two separate sentences demarcated by a full stop and capital letter. Alternatively, you could use a coordinating conjunction to join the two clauses. However, the effect would be different in each case.

The following examples are all correctly and appropriately punctuated, but the punctuation creates different effects. In the first example, the punctuation indicates a clear separation between the three sentences; in the second, the connection between the first two clauses is made clear by the coordinating conjunction 'and'. However, in the third example, the semi-colon implies a link between the first two clauses, but leaves the reader to work out what it is – that the sunshine and the birdsong combine in equal measure to create a sense of wellbeing. The final sentence clinches this.

1. The sun was shining. The birds were singing. All was well with the world.

2. The sun was shining and the birds were singing. All was well with the world.

3. The sun was shining; the birds were singing. All was well with the world.

Semi-colons can also be used to separate items in more complex lists, where commas aren't able to make the meaning sufficiently clear. Notice the semi-colon before the final 'and'.

> We saw a kingfisher flitting along the riverbank, a flash of bright blue in the sunlight; water voles nosing their way through the reed beds, heading for their burrows; and delicate dragonflies, hunting for their prey.

Compare it to the version below that uses commas throughout and see how much more difficult it is to navigate.

> We saw a kingfisher flitting along the riverbank, a flash of bright blue in the sunlight, water voles nosing their way through the reed beds, heading for their burrows, and delicate dragonflies, hunting for their prey.

Teaching about semi-colons

Few children's writers use semi-colons (J K Rowling is an exception who uses them frequently) so pupils are unlikely to encounter them in their independent reading. Since you can't rely on pupils picking them up through natural exposure, you'll need to find a few choice examples, or write some yourself. They merit direct teaching, and can be easily demonstrated in the following way:

1. Write two separate sentences on the board. (*Claire was drawing. Tom was chatting.*)
2. Model how to join the two sentences by using different conjunctions and discuss the effect. (*Claire was drawing, but Tom was chatting. Claire was drawing so Tom was chatting. Claire was drawing while Tom was chatting. Claire was drawing and Tom was chatting.*)
3. Model how to join them using a semi-colon and discuss the effect. (*Claire was drawing; Tom was chatting.*)
4. Give pupils pairs of sentences and ask them to try out the approach in small groups, discussing the effect of the semi-colon each time.
5. Ask pupils to use at least one semi-colon in their next piece of independent writing. Be sure to follow up to check that they've used it correctly.

Give pupils a passage and ask them to find one or two places where a semi-colon might be used. You could do this in small groups and give each group a different passage. Each group could then be asked to present their passage and explain their decisions.

> Sadie pushed open the door of the old shack. It was gloomy inside, and she could just make out the bulky shape covered in tarpaulin. She knew she shouldn't look. Her dad had told her to keep away. The shack was out of bounds. It had been ever since they moved here last summer. But what was the big secret they were keeping from her?

It's worth explicitly teaching pupils that conjunctive adverbs (such as however, nevertheless, consequently) typically follow a full stop or a semi-colon. When they introduce a clause following a semi-colon, they are typically followed by a comma:

- The flight to Singapore was surprisingly comfortable; however, our hotel was very disappointing.
- The flood damage to the school hall is severe; consequently, term will end a week earlier than planned.

WHEN MIGHT WE NEED TO USE SEMI-COLONS IN WRITING?

The semi-colon was widely used in the eighteenth and nineteenth centuries when long, complex sentence structures were favoured. Today the trend seems to favour shorter and less complex sentence structures, and the semi-colon is less widely used. Very few children's writers use it. However, it's a very useful punctuation mark that can convey subtleties of meaning and economy. Because the reader has to work out the link between the clauses, it supports inference and deduction, forging a closer relationship between reader and writer. Many would say that the semi-colon, effectively used, is one mark of a sophisticated writer.

What you need to know about colons

A colon is typically used to join two main clauses, with the second clause providing some explanation, elaboration or clarification of the first. Whereas a semi-colon suggests a sense of balance, a colon looks ahead to what comes next.

- The teacher knew why Paul was such an engaging writer: he had always been an avid reader.
- Tabitha peered out of the window: there was only darkness.
- There was much opposition to the new bypass: the potential damage to the countryside was just too great.

The national curriculum requires children to learn how to use colons to mark the boundary between independent clauses, and the sentences above are examples of the way they can do this. However, unlike a semi-colon, the words that follow the colon do not have to be a main clause – they may just consist of a single word. Notice that the words that precede the colon are almost always a main clause, even though the words that follow may be a phrase or just a single word.

- The school was facing a major challenge: the recruitment of a new headteacher.
- Sandra could think of only one reason for his behaviour: jealousy.

In the same way, a colon can also introduce a list. Notice again how the words that precede the colon consist of a main clause:

- I have three friends: Charlie, Sandip and Talia.
- There were strong arguments in favour of the new supermarket: convenience, greater choice and lower prices.

You'll notice that, unless the colon is introducing a quotation, the words that follow the colon do not normally start with a capital letter (unless, of course, they are proper nouns).

Remember that the words that precede the colon should usually be a main clause. The following would be incorrect:

- My best friends include: Charlie, Sandip and Talia.
- The main arguments in favour of the new supermarket were: convenience, greater choice and lower prices.

Teaching about colons

You can teach about colons through suspense writing alongside dashes and ellipsis dots as a way of hinting at what might be coming next.

Alternatively, you can tease out the subtle but important difference between the colon and the semi-colon by showing pupils how the meaning is affected by their choice of punctuation in the following way:

Begin by writing two sentences on the board:

> Billy was crying. Justine was having a tantrum.

Explain that there is no obvious connection between the events described in these two sentences. We don't know what has made Billy cry, or why Justine is having a tantrum.

Now change the full stop to a semi-colon and ask pupils to discuss the difference this makes to the meaning. You might need to tease out the way the semi-colon suggests to the reader that there is a connection between these two events, as the semi-colon implies that they are linked. However, we still don't know how – perhaps their mum has told them off or taken away a favourite toy. . .

> Billy was crying; Justine was having a tantrum.

Now change the semi-colon to a colon and ask pupils to discuss the difference this makes to the meaning. The colon suggests a different kind of connection between the two events, as the second clause now explains the first. In other words, we now know that Billy is crying because Justine is having a tantrum. Perhaps Billy is a baby and Justine has woken him with her tantrum. . .

> Billy was crying: Justine was having a tantrum.

The semi-colon and the colon certainly make the reader work out the link between the two clauses. The important next step to secure the learning is to ask pupils to write a few more sentences before or after this sentence to provide some context. Share them – or ask pupils to read them out – and see how they are supported by the choice of colon or semi-colon.

> Billy was crying; Justine was having a tantrum. The classroom was in total chaos. The new teacher was trying desperately to calm the situation.

> Billy was crying: Justine was having a tantrum. She always had to have her own way. She made his life a misery whenever he wouldn't give in to her demands. If only he'd known what she was really like before he married her. . .

WHEN MIGHT WE NEED TO USE COLONS IN WRITING?

Colons fulfil a very useful function in writing, supporting cohesion in the way they point ahead to subsequent explanation, elaboration or clarification.

Punctuation

What you need to know about speech punctuation

We use direct speech when we want to show the actual spoken words used by a character. The rules for doing this are quite clear:

1. The spoken words are enclosed by a pair of inverted commas (or speech marks). These might be single or double, but the important thing is to be consistent.

2. A reporting clause typically introduces the spoken words, but it can be placed at the end, or in the middle of the spoken words.

3. A capital letter is used at the beginning of the spoken words, unless it's a continuation of a sentence that's been interrupted by a reporting clause in mid-position. The reporting clause only begins with a capital letter when it starts a sentence.

4. A comma (or other punctuation, such as a question mark, an exclamation mark or ellipsis dots) separates the spoken words from the reporting clause. It is always placed inside the closing inverted commas.

5. If there is no reporting clause, a full stop (or other 'end' punctuation) is placed inside the closing inverted commas.

> My teacher said, 'We're going to do some work on the Vikings this term.'
>
> 'We're going to do some work on the Vikings this term,' said my teacher.
>
> 'We're going to do some work on the Vikings this term,' said my teacher, 'so I'd like you to do some research.'
>
> 'We're going to do some work on the Vikings this term,' said my teacher. 'Does anybody know who the Vikings were?'

You also need to be aware of the following:

-   In extended dialogue, you can omit the reporting clause as long as the reader can work out who is speaking.
-   You should start a new line for each change of speaker.
-   You can use a colon to introduce speech in a play script.
-   Dialogue in play scripts and in speech bubbles doesn't need inverted commas.

Teaching about speech punctuation

There are plenty of opportunities to look at the way speech is represented in books, from picture books for young children through to novels for older children that use extended dialogue.

You might introduce speech punctuation by using speech bubbles. Look at a comic or graphic novel, or produce some simple speech bubbles of your own. Explain that the words in the bubbles are the words that are actually spoken by the characters. You could ask children to write a short narrative that consists entirely of speech bubbles, or they could make a storyboard based on a traditional tale. Another effective way is to show a page from a picture book on the whiteboard and insert speech bubbles around each character for pupils to complete.

You can develop this work by giving pupils a short passage that includes dialogue without speech marks and asking them to underline the spoken words. You can then move on to model how to enclose those words in speech marks.

The rules for punctuating speech are relatively straightforward, and one of the best ways to really secure children's understanding of them is to use an investigative approach. Give children different examples of punctuated speech – or ask them to find examples in a range of books from your classroom or library. They'll need enough examples for the conventions to become apparent. Ask them, in small groups, to agree a set of rules based on their observations.

You might support their research with some prompts:

- How do we show which words are spoken?
- What happens if the spoken words are interrupted by some unspoken words?
- What do you notice about where the comma goes?

This could easily take a whole lesson. The agreed class rules can be displayed and reinforced whenever children are writing dialogue.

With older pupils, you might look at a page of extended dialogue in a novel and discuss the way the reporting clauses are sometimes omitted. Ask pupils to consider why they think the writer has done this, and whether they can still work out who is speaking. Tease out the importance of the 'new speaker, new line' convention, perhaps by highlighting the different speakers in different colours.

Older pupils can also be shown how to change direct speech into indirect (or reported) speech. Explain that a mixture of direct and indirect speech can make writing more interesting, and consider when reported speech might be more appropriate. Newspaper reports typically combine both forms.

> John Smith (85) said that he saw the van drive off at speed. 'They were certainly in a hurry, whoever they were,' he said.

WHEN MIGHT WE NEED TO USE SPEECH PUNCTUATION IN WRITING?

We need to use speech punctuation whenever we write dialogue. For example, in a narrative or short story that uses dialogue to convey character, establish the setting or move the action forwards.

What you need to know about bullet points

Bullet points are a relatively recent form of punctuation, and the advent of word-processing has increased their use in print over recent years. As such, there are no clearly defined rules for their use. There are some conventions, however, and these are largely set out in various style guides. Some guides advocate the simplest punctuation possible, whereas others see a bulleted list as a vertical sentence that requires standard sentence punctuation. The one thing that seems to be unanimously agreed is that, whichever choice you make, you should use it consistently.

Here are some generally agreed conventions:

- Bullet points can consist of single words, phrases, clauses, sentences or even short paragraphs.
- Single words or phrases may or may not begin with a capital letter, and they are not usually demarcated by a full stop. However, some style guides advocate the use of a full stop after only the final bullet, while others require a semi-colon after each bullet and a full stop after the final bullet.
- A bullet that consists of a complete sentence (or more than one sentence) begins with a capital letter and ends in a full stop.
- Any introductory words are likely to be followed by a colon. If the introductory words form a stem (rather than a main clause), the bullets must follow on from it grammatically and make sense.
- Bullets in a list should be consistent in style (single words or phrases, or sentences, but not a mixture).

We should remember that the main purpose of bullet points is to help the reader find their way around a text and locate information quickly and easily. For this reason, it makes sense to avoid a 'heavy' punctuation style, and to opt for a minimal approach to punctuation where possible.

Any of the following would be perfectly acceptable:

Please bring the following on sports day: • Sports kit • Towel • Sun cream • Sun hats/sun glasses • Bottle of water	The apostrophe is used in two ways: • To show where letters have been missed out in a contraction; • To show that something belongs to someone or something.
Here are some interesting facts about earthquakes: • Earthquakes are triggered by the movement of the earth's plates. • Some earthquakes go unnoticed. • Earthquakes can trigger other natural disasters, such as tsunamis and landslides.	We stay safe in science lessons by doing the following things: • Wearing goggles and an apron • Tying back long hair • Not touching or tasting any substances • Washing our hands at the end of the lesson • Being careful and following instructions

Teaching about bullet points

Bullet points are best taught alongside other presentational devices, such as headings, sub-headings, columns and tables.

You could give pupils a selection of information texts that use bullet points and ask them to agree a class set of conventions for their use.

You could give pupils an unformatted information text and ask them to work in pairs or small groups to decide how best to present the content. They would need to agree how to use layout features such as headings, sub-headings, paragraphs or sections, tables, columns, fact boxes and bullet points. You could link this to work in history or geography.

Alternatively, ask pupils to work in groups to research information about a given topic. Once they've gathered relevant material, ask them to think about the different presentational devices they might use to present their findings in the form of an information leaflet or a page for a school text book. They could plan the layout before populating it with their findings.

Heading	
<u>Sub-heading</u> **Text**	**Picture with caption**
Did you know. . .? • • •	<u>Sub-heading</u> **Text**

WHEN MIGHT WE NEED TO USE BULLET POINTS IN WRITING?

We might choose to use bullet points when we're looking for a layout that is clear and easy to navigate. If we want our reader to retrieve chunks of information quickly and easily, typically in information texts, bullet points should be considered.

Glossary of grammatical terms

Active voice	The most frequently used 'voice' whereby the subject of the verb and the 'doer' (agent) are one and the same. The active voice places the focus on the 'doer' (agent).
Adjective	A word that modifies or gives more information about a noun or a pronoun.
Adverb	A word that modifies a verb, an adjective or another adverb. Adverbs can tell us about time, frequency, duration, place, manner and degree.
Adverbial	A word, phrase or clause that functions adverbially, typically to modify a verb or a clause.
Antonym	A word that has the opposite meaning to another word.
Article	A type of determiner. There are two types of article: the definite article (*the*) and the indefinite articles (*a/an*).
Auxiliary verb	A type of verb used in front of a lexical verb to modify its meaning. The primary auxiliary verbs are *be*, *do* and *have*.
Clause	Part of a sentence typically containing a subject, a verb and any additional words or phrases that complete the meaning. Clauses can be main or subordinate.
Cohesion	The way a text is woven together, typically through the use of devices that operate as signposts for the reader, signalling how different parts of a text relate to each other.
Conjunction	A word that joins words, phrases or clauses. There are two types: coordinating conjunctions and subordinating conjunctions.
Contracted form	The compression of two or more words into one, with the omitted letters replaced by an apostrophe.
Determiner	A word that specifies (or determines) a noun.
Ellipsis	The omission of words to avoid unnecessary repetition.
Finite verb	A verb that indicates tense.
Gerund	A verb ending in –ing that functions as a noun, e.g. *swimming*, *eating* etc.
Grapheme	A unit of the writing system, typically a letter or group of letters.

Head	The key word in a phrase. The head of a noun phrase is the single noun that is modified by the other words in the noun phrase.
Imperative	A 'mood' that expresses directive meaning (such as commands).
Infinitive	The base form of a verb, often preceded by 'to'.
Irregular verb	A verb that does not conform to the regular inflected form, typically in the simple past and the –ed form (past participle).
Lexical verb	A type of verb that is not an auxiliary or a modal verb. It is sometimes referred to as a 'content' verb.
Minor sentence	A sentence that doesn't contain a verb.
Modal verb	A particular type of auxiliary verb that expresses an attitude such as possibility, certainty, necessity or ability.
Modification	The addition of extra detail before (pre-modification) or after (post-modification) a word, phrase or clause.
Mood	The writer's attitude as indicated by the verb form. There are three 'moods': the indicative mood, which expresses factual meaning; the imperative mood, which expresses directive meaning; and the subjunctive mood, which expresses unfulfilled or desired states, events or actions as well as compulsion or necessity.
Morpheme	The smallest grammatical unit that carries meaning in a word. The word 'disagreement' consists of three morphemes: 'dis', 'agree' and 'ment'.
Non-finite clause	A type of subordinate clause that takes a non-finite (or non-tensed) verb.
Noun	A word that names a thing, a person, a place, a feeling, a quality or an idea.
Noun phrase	A group of words with a noun or pronoun as its 'head'.
Object	The person or thing affected by the action of the verb. There are direct objects and indirect objects.
Parenthesis	A word or group of words inserted into a sentence as a kind of afterthought, usually punctuated by a pair of brackets, dashes or commas. (The term 'parentheses' can also be used to describe a pair of brackets.)
Participle	The –ing and –ed non-finite verb forms, sometimes referred to as the present and past participles.
Passive voice	The less frequently used 'voice' whereby the subject of the verb is the recipient of the action. The passive tends to place less focus on the agent (which is sometimes omitted) and more on the actual action or event. The passive is typically formed from the appropriate tense of the verb 'be' plus the –ed form (past participle) of the main verb.
Perfect	A verb form that indicates when an action was started or completed. The present perfect is formed from 'have' plus the –ed form (past participle) of a main verb and indicates an action or event that started in the past but continues in (or continues to be relevant to) the present time. The past perfect is formed from 'had' plus the –ed form (past participle) of a main verb and indicates an action that started in the past and continued to another point in the past.

Phrase   A group of words acting as a grammatical unit and typically forming part of a clause. There are different types of phrase, such as preposition phrases and noun phrases.

Preposition   A word that indicates the relationship between things, people or events, typically in terms of time or place.

Preterite   Another name for the simple past.

Progressive   A verb form that indicates an action in progress, either in the past or the present tense. It is formed from the appropriate tense of the auxiliary verb 'be' plus the –ing form of a main (lexical) verb.

Pronoun   A word that stands in (like a substitute) for a noun or noun phrase.

Relative clause A type of subordinate clause that post-modifies a noun, a noun phrase, a clause or a whole sentence.

Relative pronoun A type of pronoun used to introduce a relative clause.

Sentence   A group of words typically containing at least one main clause. In writing, a sentence is demarcated by a capital letter and a full stop. Sentences can function as statements, questions, exclamations or commands.

Simple form   A verb form used to indicate the simple present or simple past. The simple present is formed from the base form of the verb (the –s form is used to form the third-person singular). The simple past is formed from the –ed form of the verb (irregular verbs take other forms).

Standard English The dialect that is generally used for formal purposes in speech and writing, carrying a clear element of social and academic prestige.

Subject   The person or thing that performs the action of the verb.

Subjunctive   A 'mood' that expresses unfulfilled or desired states, events or actions as well as compulsion or necessity. It is associated with very formal – and sometimes archaic – writing.

Synonym   A word that has the same (or a similar) meaning to another word.

Tense   The use of a particular verb form to indicate the time frame of an event or action.

Verb   A word that indicates action or a state of being.

Voice   The way information is presented in a clause. Writers have a choice of two 'voices' – active or passive.

Word class   A group of words that function in the same way, such as nouns, adjectives or determiners.

Further reading

Ronald Carter and Michael McCarthy, *Cambridge Grammar of English* (Cambridge: Cambridge University Press, 2006)

David Crystal, *Rediscover Grammar* (London: Longman, 1988)

David Crystal, *Making a Point* (London: Profile Books, 2015)

John Seely, *Oxford A–Z of Grammar & Punctuation* (Oxford: Oxford University Press, 2004)

R L Trask, *Penguin Guide to Punctuation* (London: Penguin Books, 1997)